OTHER RELIGIONS OF THE WORLD

OTHER RELIGIONS OF THE WORLD

PRAMOTE SEANGPOLSIT

GYAN PUBLISHING HOUSE
NEW DELHI-110002

Other Religions of the World

ISBN : 81-212-0955-2
Rs. 540

Published in 2007 in India by
Gyan Publishing House,
5, Ansari Road, Daryaganj, New Delhi-110002
Phones : 23282060, 23261060
Fax : (011) 23285914
E-mail : books@gyanbooks.com
Website : www.gyanbooks.com

Laser Type-setting by : Shagun Graphics, Delhi
Printed at : Salasar Imaging System, Delhi

CONTENTS

Messages

Religion plays the most important role in man's life. It makes the life of a man worthy and peaceful. If a man follows the true message of religion, he can, definitely, reach the goal of life.

Assistant Professor Pramote Seangpolsit in his book, "OTHER RELIGIONS OF THE WORLD" has discusses with length about those religions of the world which are not much known in the general people. He has tried to explain the fundamentals of these religions in a beautiful manner, and I believe that this work will receive good response from readers and scholars.

I extend my best wishes to the author and for the success of his work.

-Prof. Dr. M. Shahidul Huq Munshi
Head,
Department of Political Science
University of Dhaka, Bangladesh

Messages

I am glad to know that Assistant Professor Pramote Seangpolsit, Director of Suan Dusit Rajabhat University, Suphanburi (Thailand) is bringing out a thought-provoking book under the title 'Other Religions of the World.'

As the religion is a perennial source of illumination, I have great appreciation for Professor Pramote's book on religions and extend my best wishes for the success of this well-prepared book, and the author for his scholarship.

-Dr. L. M. Singhvi
Formerly Indian High Commissioner in U. K.

Messages

I am happy to learn that Professor Pramote Seangpolsit, Director, Suan Dusit Rajabhat University, Suphanburi, Thailand has written a book on Other Religions of the World.

I am sure this work will focus on fundamentals of religions and will be of great inspiration to the people in terms of love, brotherhood, unity and peace, irrespective of cast, creed and community, for which the whole world is looking.

I wish the effort of the author all success.

University of Odense
Odense, Denmark

-Prof. Dr. Niels Thomassen

FOREWORD

From the very beginning of man's life, the Religion (DHARMA) has played a key role in his daily behaviours and progress. In its broad meaning, the Religion (DHARMA) is adoption of goodness; it carries with it the spirit of all-welfare. What we take to be religions on the earth are, in fact, religious-communities and each of them directs its followers to lead life in a separate way based on some eternal value foremostly. Because that eternal value also incorporates goodness in it, all religious-communities become an indispensable part of religion, no matter if the scope of them is not vast.

It is matter of pleasure and satisfaction that Professor Pramote Seangpolsit has prepared a manuscript from the fundamentals of those religious-communities, which are not much known, under the title, "OTHER RELIGIONS OF THE WORLD." I believe that after publication of it, all interested will learn a lot about the subject.

I wish Professor Pramote Seangpolsit and his endeavours all success.

GUJARAT (India)

—D.D. Jadeja
Ex. Vice Chancellor
Sardar Patel University

INTRODUCTION

Our world, since the emergence of human beings has been under the influence of the concept of Supreme power. The driving forces of nature have always fascinated humans. The first ones among them had been the floods, earthquakes, draughts and volcano eruptions. The early simple humans had always taken these things as natural calamities bestowed upon them by the supreme powers as a punishment of their sins. This concept later gave birth to the concept of religion. The rising and setting of the sun along with the waning and waxing of the moon added to a great deal of fascination in the hearts of these simple humans and they began wondering on such natural acts with great curiosity.

As we are now well aware of the fact that every religion shares the concept of Heaven and Hell, the doctrine of salvation in a Heaven and also of damnation in a Hell form an important part of every religion. Such bliss and such a misery may be said to be eternal as in Christianity and Islam, while it may be said to be for a limited period of time as it is with Hinduism and Buddhism. This concept is based on the supposition that some part of our personality exists even after death to let us enjoy the pleasures or to let us bear the sufferings through Heaven and Hell. This added to the general acceptance of the religion. If we go back in time thinking of the early nomadic life of humans, we find that the desires and requirements of people were very limited at that time. They lived a contented life and were happy with the well being of their cattle. They searched for the green pastures and dwelt near them for a long time.

Later, with the increase in population, people began thinking of their own private property to keep them and their family safe with heaps of grain and with private pastures for their cattle. This further added to the struggle between the people owning larger properties and the people with smaller assets. This was the time when people began thinking of pleasing the Supreme powers of nature for deriving personal benefits.

To help people in this act of pleasing powers, certain wizards came into existence that claimed to be in contact with the cosmic powers. This group of people neither had their own cattle herds nor they cultivated the land. They only helped the people in satisfying the forces of nature for their personal benefit and in return they were granted all the things necessary for living. These were the first persons that added to the complexity of religion and introduced the concept of soul to it. At that time many superstitious beliefs added to it and people started believing that the dead person had some kind of existence and authority even after death.

When this concept became popular and people started worrying about their well being after death, the Heaven and Hell came into light. Their basic role was to stop people from struggling over worldly things. It was declared that after death, the soul of every good person reaches Heaven and of every bad person reaches Hell. Heaven was described to be a place where every person got everything he wished for and hell was a place where the sinners were punished. Every religion of the world has scriptures related to this concept that speak of different accounts and deal with full details. The early people living in the Middle East always desired of the big green pastures and huge cattle folks and it is therefore that the Bible describes Heaven as a place where rivers of milk and honey flow. Similarly, because of the hard livelihood in several regions of Asia, the Heaven was described as a place where no one had to work for and still there are all the riches and beautiful girls to serve them.

Although the purpose of a religion has always been this thought that is the hidden thirst of every soul:

'From the unreal lead us to the Real,

From darkness lead us to the Light,

From death lead us to Immortality.'

But due to the attraction and curiosity of attaining such pleasures, people became very conscious about their welfare and devoted themselves to certain religious deeds that were said to be helping the performer in attaining Heaven. The religious scriptures gave detailed account of the other methods of attaining Heaven too. The most common among them was performing only good deeds in social and family life. In this way, the religion even helped people to live peaceful lives among the other members of the village or society.

Now we can define religion as a person's attitude towards the unseen and the forces driving the nature, and whatever consequences his belief or attitude produces on his conduct or on his relations to his other fellow men. Darwin, in the 'Descent of Man,' Part I., chap. iii, describes the feeling of religious devotion as a highly complex one, consisting of love, complete submission to an exalted and mysterious superior, a strong sense of dependence, fear, reverence, gratitude, hope for the future. But other than this thought, there are num-erous superstitions, customs and practices associated with such beliefs. Since ancient times and even till present day, every religion has been affected by such practices. Although the shape and nature of them has altered with time, still they stand on the same foundations when human sacrifices, trials by ordeal, witchcraft and sorcery that were said to grant the person whatever he wished.

In modern times, majority of people seek fortune to satisfy the lust for materialism. For this purpose they follows the teachings of their native religion. Some religions say that reciting so and so scripture brings good luck; some say that going to so and so places brings auspiciousness to life. Whether methods are different and change with change of culture and religion, still the root cause behind such a mental process is a person's insecurity and his desire for personal well being.

Still in some religions, a dead ancestor is considered to possess the power to bestow fortune upon a family he belonged. The main reason behind such a thought is that the person who had died had entered into some unknown realms where supernatural powers exist and if he wished, he could bless and bring happiness to other members of the family too.

People had always been curious to solve the mystery of death. The general belief regarding that had always been the detachment of something from the body after death. But as it is just a belief, the darkness of doubt has always covered it on the beginning and at the end, as also hinted by Shakespeare in the following lines from his famous play 'The Tempest':

'Yea, all which it inherit, shall dissolve
And, like this insubstantial pageant faded,
Leave not a rack behind; we are such stuff
As dreams are made on, and our little life
Is rounded with a sleep.'

This quest for the unknown, this curiosity for the hidden gave opportunity to a small segment of society who claimed to have solved this mystery. This segment was of the wizards, the so-called holy men. So, when the wizards came into light and declared that they had the answers to all the questions, people were bound to get attracted. But because of the absence of writing, this wizard was like a living book keeping in memory, the details of all the legends, customs, and legal codes and above all the principles of getting connected to the cosmic through souls.

And on comparing all the religions of the world whether ancient or modern, we find that all the above said characteristics are present in all of them. And despite this fact, some religions have stood upright on time's scale, against all odds while some others have disappeared in the course of time. It cannot be doubted that there have been forms of religion that have left no records. But even those who survive in records, or in actual existence, are numerous and only a brief review of some of them is possible. Still on reviewing the available records and characteristics, we find that there are various mystical elements that are common in several ancient religions. Such as in Egypt, India and Mexico, all the divine beings of the pantheon are pictured as either holding a serpent in the hand or on forehead. This might be true that it had some connection with the mystical serpent power that even in present day attracts the attention of the people in search of some spiritual power. Although the Egyptian and the Mexican culture have been a thing of the past but Indian culture till date has well preserved the secrets of this mystic science. There are several books written on the most common and widely accepted religions of the world. Though each religion has its own peculiar growth, the seed from which they had sprung is almost the same everywhere. But I have tried to find out the details of the cultural backgrounds, rituals and social effects of the lesser-known religions of the world that have either disappeared or have a small number of people following them still. It is true in the general affairs of human life and in religion that there is a need of movement, circulation and change for the continuation of life. From the earliest conception of a creative force in the animal and vegetable world to the latest development in Esotericism, there has never been anything that might be termed as a new religion. I have tried to find out the circumstances of their growth and decline, their good and bad effects, their role in shaping the lives of people, their root concept and of course their views on the cosmic. As the earliest conceptions of a God lie buried beneath ages of corruption and in the glimpses of the earlier faiths of mankind.

I wish to convey my heartiest regards to Prof. D.D.Jadeja, Ex. Vice Chancellor, Sardar Patel University, Gujarat, India, who not only has encouraged me to prepare this manuscript, but has been kind enough to contribute a foreword to it.

My special thanks are also due to my colleague Dr. Paitoon Patyaiying for his continous support and encouragement.

Although it is an undeniable truth that man created his own gods; yet they are now powerless to change them. I wish to conclude with an ancient Buddhist saying:

'While eating and fighting,
Man resembles a beast,
It is only the religion that makes the difference.'

I hope this book will sketch a true picture of these religions that had not only affected the lives of the people following them but also had an effect on other neighbouring cultures.

—*Pramote Seangpolsit*

CHAPTER-1

INCA

The Sun has been one of the major Deities of the ancient world irrespective of the fact that all the religions had extremely different factors responsible for their development through the ages. Sun has always been an object of curiosity because of its rising and setting at the horizon. Its incomparable brightness has always drawn the attention of even the earliest living beings on this earth. This same sun was the major God of the Incas (the followers of Inca religion) too.

Of all the nations occupying the American continent at the time of the discovery made by the Europeans, the two most advanced in power and refinement of all those were the nations of Mexico and Peru. It was due to the contribution of the Aztecs that Mexican civilization rose so high in architecture and religious concepts. While on the other hand we have the Incas, who shaped the hardships of the Andes mountain range according to their own need, giving the American continent one of the best-cultured and most religious civilization of the world. The empire of Peru, at the time of Spanish invasion, stretched along the coast of the Pacific Ocean.

The roots of this civilization were in the valley of Cuzco, which is the most central region of Peru, in southern America. Their most important cult was directed to Inti, the Sun God who was said to nourish the earth and man with his rays. The word Inca itself is derived from the sun god Inti and literally it means the son of the sun god. The face of the country was quite unfavourable to the purposes of agriculture and communication. But by means of the great roads passing through the mountain passes, opened an easy communication between the capital and the remotest parts of the empire.

Legends of Origin

In ancient times, when different people and tribes of the continent were indulged barbarism, they worshipped nearly every object in nature, fought with each other to prove their authority and feasted on the flesh of their captives. The Sun, the great luminary took compassion on their condition and sent two of his children namely Manco Capac and Mama Oello Huaco, as a guide and teacher to teach the natives to lead a cultured life. This pair of brother and sister, husband and wife, advanced along the high plains. They bore with them a golden wedge, and were directed by the god to take up their residence on the very spot where the sacred emblem sunk into the ground without effort. They proceeded ahead and it was at the valley of Cuzco, that the sacred emblem sank and disappeared. Here they established their residence. Manco Capac started teaching the men the methods of agriculture and cultivation while, Mama Oello taught the women about weaving. The simple people started gathering in the valley of Cuzco and thus laid the foundations of a civilization that flourished till the advent of the Spanish. The city of Cuzco situated at the centre of the valley gradually started advancing in wealth and soon became a big city, the echo of whose worth was heard in every corner of the continent. Inca believed that a host of nature deities controlled their lives and needed to be appeased by careful attention through certain special rituals and sacrifices. With respect to their customs, the Inca's weavers started making the most extraordinary cloth and the farmers raised excellent crops.

Legend Of Creation

About the creation of humans, there is a legend that is still famous among the natives. According to it, in the beginning, and before this world was created, there was a being called Viracocha. He created a dark world without sun, moon or stars. Owing to this creation he was named Viracocha Pachayachachi, which means "Creator of all things." And when he had created the world he formed a race of giants of disproportioned greatness painted and sculptured, to see whether it would be well to make real men of that size. But on seeing those sculptures, he disapproved and destroyed them. He then created men in his likeness as they are now; and they all lived in the world of darkness.

Viracocha being their Creator, ordered these people that they should live without quarrelling, and that they should know and serve him. He gave them a certain code of living to follow strictly. People kept this precept for some time, but due to the arising of the feeling of pride they broke that code. Through this sin, they invoked the anger of Viracocha and he cursed them.

Then some people were turned into stones, others into other lifeless things, some were swallowed up by the earth, others by the sea, and over all there came a general flood which they call unu pachacuti, which means "water that overturns the land." Legend says that it rained continuously for 60 days and nights and drowned all the created things with only some stone structures remaining behind as a memorial of the event.

Although this legend is most popular among the Inca population, still, some other communities dwelling away from Cuzco have another famous legend to tell. They say that at the time of the heavy flood, there was a mountain named Guasano in the province of Quito. Two brothers named Ataorupagui and Cusicayo walked up the mountain. As the water level began to rise, the mountain also kept rising and hence keeping it above in such a way that the flood did not cover it. In this way the two brothers were saved. When the water level reduced, these two, came down and began to sow in their land. One day when they returned to their hut, they found some small loaves of bread, and a jar of beverage. They did not know who had brought it, but they gave thanks to the Creator, ate the bread and drank the beverage. Next day the same thing happened again. Out of curiosity, they hid themselves to watch over for the bringers of their food. While they were watching they saw two young women preparing the eatables and putting them in the accustomed place. When they were about to depart, the men tried to seize them, but they escaped. The brothers on realising the mistake they had made in insulting those who had done them so much good, became sad and prayed to Viracocha to pardon them for their sins, asking him to let the women come back and give them the accustomed meals. The Creator granted their wish. The women came back and said to the brothers, 'The Creator has thought it well that we should return to you, unless you should die of hunger.' They brought them food. Then there was friendship between the women and the brothers, and one of the brothers got engaged with one of the women. Then, one day, the elder brother was drowned in a nearby lake and the other surviving brother married one of the women, and had the other as a concubine. By them he had ten sons who formed two lineages of five each, and increasing in numbers they called one Hanansaya that is the same as to say the upper party, and the other Hurinsaya, or the lower party. From these all the Incas that now exist are descended.

In the same way, other communities have legends of how some of their people were saved, from whom they trace their origin and descent. But the Incas and most of those of living near Cuzco, do not say that anyone escaped from the flood, but that Viracocha began to create men afresh. One thing is believed among all the nations of these parts, for they all speak generally and as well known of the general flood.

Legend of the Second Age, and Creation

There is another legend that deals with the creation of life after being destroyed by the flood. This is called the Legend of the Second Age. This can be summed up as follows:

It is well known that once during the flood, everything was destroyed. It must now be known that Viracocha, when he destroyed the land, preserved three men who might serve and help him in the creation of new people. After the flood passed and the land dried, Viracocha determined to populate it for a second time, and, to make it more perfect, he decided upon creating luminaries to give it light. With this object he went, with his servants, to a great lake in which there is an island called Titicaca, the meaning being "the rock of lead." Viracocha went to this island, and presently ordered that the sun, moon, and stars should come forth, and be set in the heavens to give light to the world, and it was done so. Legend also tells that at first, the moon was created brighter than the sun, which made the sun jealous at the time when they rose into the sky. So the sun threw a handful of ash over the moon's face, which gave it the shaded colour still present. Viracocha gave various orders to his servants, but one of them disobeyed the commands of Viracocha. So Viracocha being angry on him ordered the other two servants to take him and tie him hands and feet. When this was done, Viracocha made a sacred idol in that place, as a place for worship and as a sign of what he had created there.

Leaving the island, he passed by the lake to the main land, taking with him the two servants who survived. He went to a place now called *Tiahuanacu* in the province of Collasuyu, and in this place he designed all the nations on a rock, that he desired to create. This done, he ordered his two servants to charge their memories with the names of all tribes that he had depicted, and of the valleys and provinces where they were to come forth, which were those of the whole land. He ordered that each one should go by a different road and name different tribes. He also ordered them to populate the country. The servants, obeying the command of Viracocha, set out on their journey and work. One went by the mountain range, the other went by the heights which overlook the wonderful mountain ranges which we call the Andes, situated to the east of the sea. By these roads they went, saying with a loud voice, "Oh you tribes and nations, hear and obey the order of Viracocha, who commands you to go forth, and multiply and settle the land." Viracocha himself did the same along the road between those taken by his two servants, naming all the tribes and places by which he passed. Every place obeyed at the call of his voice and people came forth, some from lakes, others from fountains, valleys, caves, trees, rocks and hills, spreading over the land and multiplying to form nations which are found in Peru today.

Whether it was in one way or the other, all the legends agree that Viracocha was the creator of these people. They have the tradition that he was a man of medium height, white and dressed in a white robe like an alb secured round the waist, and that he carried a staff and a book in his hands.

And though he was paid respect in every place he went, still there is a legend that tells of a strange event. It says that Viracocha, after creating all the people, went on his road and came to a place where many men of his creation had assembled. When Viracocha arrived there, the inhabitants suspected him due to his dress and bearing. They murmured at him and proposed to throw him from a hill that was near. They took their weapons there, and gathered together with evil intentions against Viracocha. He fell on his knees on the ground and clasped his hands clasped, fire came down on the hill, and covered all the place, burning up the earth and stones like straw. Those bad men were terrified at the fearful fire. They came down from the hill, and sought pardon from Viracocha for their sin. Viracocha was moved by their request. He went to the flames and put them out with his staff.

After this Viracocha continued his journey and arrived at a place called Urcos, south of Cuzco. Staying there for some days, he was well served by the natives of that neighbourhood. At the time of his departure, he made them a celebrated statue, for them to offer gifts to and worship. This same statue was offered many rich gifts of gold and other metals, and above all a golden bench later by the Incas.

Viracocha continued his journey working his miracles and instructing his created beings. In this way he reached the territory on the equinoctial line and here his servants also joined him. Intending to leave the land of Peru, he made a speech to those he had created, prophesying them of the things that would happen. He told them that people would come, who would say that they were Viracocha their creator, and that they were not to believe them; but that in the time to come he would send his messengers who would protect and teach them. Having said this he went to sea with his two servants, and went travelling over the water as if it was land, without sinking. For they appeared like foam over the water, and the people, therefore, gave them the name of Viracocha that means 'the grease or foam of the sea.'

The Incas, like so many other Indian races, believed in a Supreme Being, the Creator and Ruler of the Universe, whom they called using different names of Pachacamac and Viracocha. Pachacamac literally means, 'He who sustains or gives life to the universe' and it was an epithet of the creator. While Viracocha means 'the foam of the sea.' Pachacamac also sometimes expressed the name of the great deity and Viracocha combined. But the deity whose worship Incas never forgot, wherever or to whatever extent their empire boundaries extended, was the Sun. It was he, who, gave light and warmth to the nations, and life to the crops; whom they considered as the father of the royal dynasty, the founder of the empire; and whose temples were built in every city and were found in almost every village throughout the empire, while the altars smoked with burnt offerings, a form of sacrifice peculiar to the Incas among the semi-civilized nations of the New World. The deities were offered prayers daily and they formed and inseparable part of the life of a common Inca. The thought and imagination that flows in these prayers reveals the status enjoyed by these deities in the hearts of common people. Here the translation of a few is being given:

I. TO VIRACOCHA

Viracocha, Lord of the Universe!
Whether male or female,
at any rate commander of heat and reproduction,
being one who,
even with His spittle, can work sorcery;
Where are You?
Would that You were not hidden from this son of yours!
He may be above;
He may be below;
or far away in space.
Where is his mighty judgment thronc?
He may be spread abroad among the upper waters;
or, among the lower waters and their sands
He may be dwelling.
Creator of the world,
Creator of man,
great among my ancestors,
before You my eyes fail me,
you I long to see You;
for, seeing You,
knowing You,
learning from You,
understanding You,
I shall be seen by You,
and You will know me.
The Sun—the Moon;

The Day—the Night;
summer—Winter;
not in vain,
in orderly succession,
do they march to their destined place,
to their goal.
They arrive
wherever
your royal staff,
you bear.
Oh! Listen to me,
let me not fall
that I grow weary
and die.

II. TO VIRACOCHA

O conquering Viracocha!
Ever-present Viracocha!
You who are equal upon the earth!
You who are from the beginnings of the creation until its end!
You gave life and valour to men, saying,
"Let this be a man."
And to woman, saying
"Let this be a woman."
You made them and gave them being.
Watch over them, that they may live in health and in peace.
You who are in the highest heavens,
and among the clouds of the tempest,
grant them long life,

and accept this our sacrifice,
O Creator.

III. TO PACHACAMAC

O Pachacamac!
You who have existed from the beginning,
you who shall exist until the end,
powerful but merciful,
who did create man by saying,
'Let man be,'
Who defend us from evil,
and preserve our life and our health,
are you in the sky or upon the earth?
In the clouds or in the deep water?
Hear the voice of him who calls You,
and grant him his wishes.
Give us life everlasting,
preserve us, and accept this our sacrifice.

As it is clear from these few verses that Viracocha was believed to possess supernatural powers and it was due to this belief that common people felt his power working behind every natural process. He was considered to be the father of all human beings and also as creator of all heavenly objects. In the second place was the Sun god and besides him, the Incas worshipped other objects that were in some way connected to the Sun. The Moon was among them, who were worshipped as the sister-wife of the Sun. Then there were the stars as the heavenly companions of the Moon. While it is true that the fairest and the most pleasant among the stars was Venus who was known to the Incas by the name of 'Chasca' and was described as a 'youth with the long and curling locks,' and was adored as the page of the Sun, whom he attended so closely in his rising and setting. The Thunder and Lightning, also managed to attract their attention and hence some temples were built in their name too. Rainbow was also worshipped as a beautiful image of their God.

Other than these, all the natural elements, the wind, the air, the mountains and the rivers were considered of bearing some effect on the destiny and luck of the people. But their system, although being confined to all these gods and goddesses, even absorbed the rituals and concepts of other religions when the people following them, were conquered by the Incas, whose image idols were brought directly to the capital as a symbol of victory.

But the worship of Sun was always an object of their lavish expenditure. The most ancient of the many temples dedicated to Sun were on the Island of Titicaca, from where the royal founders of the Incas were said to have proceeded. The interior of the temple was always the most worthy of admiration. It was in true words a mine of gold. The western wall was painted with a representation of the Sun, consisting of a human figure, looking forward from amid innumerable rays of light, which emerged from it in every direction. The figure was engraved on a massive plate of gold of enormous dimensions, thickly studded with emeralds and precious stones. It was so situated in front of the great eastern portal, that the rays of the morning sun fell directly upon it at its rising, lighting up the whole apartment that seemed more than natural, and which was reflected back from the golden ornaments with which the walls and ceiling were everywhere decorated. Gold, in the common mythological language of the people, was 'the tears wept by the sun'. Adjoining the principal structure were several chapels of smaller dimensions. One of them was devoted to the Moon, who was considered as the mother of the Incas. Her image was decorated in the same manner as that of the Sun but this plate and all the decorations were of silver maybe because this metal suited well with silvery light of the beautiful heavenly object. There were three other chapels, one of which was dedicated to the Stars, who formed the bright court of companions of the Sister of the Sun, another was devoted to the Thunder and the Lightning; and a third, to the Rainbow, whose many-coloured appearance was imaged on the walls with hues almost as radiant as its own. There were besides several other buildings, or insulated apartments, for the accommodation of the numerous priests who officiated in the services of the temple.

All the plates, the ornaments, and the utensils that were used in performing the rituals were also made of gold or silver. Twelve immense vases of silver stood on the floor of the great saloon, filled with grain. The censers for the perfumes, the ewers which held the water for sacrifice, the pipes which conducted it through channels into the buildings, the reservoirs that received it, even the agricultural implements used in the gardens of the temple, were all made of gold and silver. The gardens, belonging to the royal palaces were sparkled with flowers of gold and silver, and various imitations of the vegetable kingdom. Animals, also, were to be found there among which the llama, with its golden fleece, was most common, built in the same style, and with a degree of skill. Besides the great temple of the Sun, there were a large number of inferior temples and religious houses in the capital. It was the city devoted to the Sun, where his worship was maintained in all its splendour; where every fountain, pathway, and wall was regarded as a holy mystery. And any noble who, at some period or other of his life, had not made his pilgrimage to the Incan Mecca of the great temple was considered as unfortunate.

At the head of all, both here and throughout the land, stood the great High Priest, or Villac Vmu, as he was called. He was second only to the Inca king in dignity, and was usually chosen from his brothers or his nearest family members. He was appointed by the monarch, and held his office for life. It was he who then chose his subordinates for other cities. The members, who officiated in the temple of the Sun in Cuzco, were taken exclusively from the sacred race of the Incas. But the office of high priest in each district was reserved for one of the royal blood. It was designed by this regulation to preserve the faith in its purity.

The Virgins of the Sun

The great temple at Cuzco consisted wholly of maidens of the royal blood, who amounted, it is said, to about fifteen hundred. The provincial convents were supplied from the daughters of the inferior nobles, and occasionally a girl from the lower classes of the people was also recommended because of her great personal attractions. The 'Houses of the Virgins of the Sun,' as they were called, consisted of low ranges of stone buildings, covering a large extent of ground, surrounded by high walls, in which the residents were confined totally restricted from any outer observation. They were provided with every accommodation for the fair inmates, and lived in the same royal manner as the palaces of the Incas,. and the temples; for they received the particular care of government, as an important part of the religious establishment.

Though they were named the Virgins of the Sun, still they were the brides of the king, and, at a marriageable age, the most beautiful among them were selected for the honours of his bed. The full number of such girls rose by time not only to hundreds, but thousands, who all found accommodations in his different palaces throughout the country.

No one but the Inca king, and the Coya or queen, might enter the consecrated temple premises. A great attention was paid to the morals of the Virgins in service to the Sun temple, and visitors were sent every year to inspect the institutions, and to report on the state of their discipline. If ever a girl was detected in an intrigue, by the stern law of the Incas, she was to be buried alive, her lover was to be strangled, and the town or village to which he belonged was to be razed to the ground, as if to efface every memorial of its existence.

The Incas practiced daily offering and sacrifices. The human and animal sacrifices were held only on special occasions such as a festival or during the coronation of the king, when 200 children would be killed, or in times of crises such as famine, or epidemics. Children, before being sacrificed, were feasted 'so that they would not enter the presence of the gods hungry and crying.' The critical situations of natural calamities were actually considered, as a result of the disobedience to the gods and would therefore call for confession of sins. People believed that by confessing they would prevent private and public disasters. In the beginning these confessions were done in public but became secret after some time.

Many sacrifices were practiced daily for the ritual of the sun's appearance. For that purpose, a fire was kindled, and corn was thrown on the coals and toasted. 'Eat this, Lord Sun,' were the words of officiating priests, 'so that you will know that we are your children.' While on the first day of every lunar month 100 pure-white llamas were driven into the Great Square in Cuzco; they were moved about to the various images of the gods and then assigned to 30 priestly attendants, each representing a day of the month. The llamas were then sacrificed; chunks of flesh were thrown onto the fire, and the bones were powdered for ritual use. The cloaks of excellent weave were burned in the offering. The Inca ruler wore his cloaks only once and they were ceremoniously sacrificed in fire each day.

All the four principal festivals of the year were devoted to the Sun, and symbolized the great periods of his annual progress. And the most magnificent and important of all was the feast of Raymi, held at the period of the summer, when the Sun, having touched the southern extremity of his course, retraced his path, as if to gladden the hearts of his chosen people by his presence. On this occasion, the Indian nobles from the different corners and directions of the country came to the capital in huge numbers to take part in the great religious celebration.

The Festival of the Sun

The word Raymi, among the Incas was equivalent to the word Easter among the Christians. Among the four festivals that the King celebrated in the city of Cuzco, it was on the festival of Raymi that the state spent most lavishly. And it was also considered the most important because it was in the honour of the Sun. It was held during the month of June. In local language, it was called Yntip Raymi, which means the 'Solemn Feast of the Sun.' They celebrated this festival of the Sun god, in acknowledgment that they adored Him as the sole and universal power who, by his light and energy, creates and cherishes all things on earth; and that He was the natural father of the first Inca and his wife, and of all their descendants, who were sent to this earth for the benefit of all people.

All the chief nobles, lords and knights who were then not employed in war, came from all the far and near parts of the empire to attend the festival. They did so not because they were ordered to do that but because they just felt pleasure in taking part in such a great festival. Also, as the ceremonies included the worship of the Sun God and of the Inca King, there was no one who did not desire to take part in it. If nobles were somehow prevented from being present, by old age or sickness, or by the public service or the long distance, they sent their sons and brothers, to be at the festival in their place. It was considered so important.

The opening ceremonies were performed by the king himself, working as a High Priest. Although there had always been a High Priest of the royal blood, who was the uncle or brother of the Inca king, yet the king himself officiated at this great festival, as the first-born of the Sun.

All the attendants of the festival dressed in their best and newest clothes, and the Indian lords and nobles competed with each other in the display of costly ornaments and jewels, while canopies borne by attendants over their heads, gave to the great square, and the streets that emptied into it, an appearance of being spread over with one vast and magnificent spirit. Some people came in a simple costume - wrapped in the skins of lions, with the heads fixed over their own. These were the Indians who claimed descent from a lion. The common people brought instruments in their hands, such as flutes and tambourines, and pieces of skin, to assist them in their fooleries. Other nobles wore various costumes to distinguish them, and each different tribe came with the arms with which they fought in war. Some had bows and arrows; others lances, darts, javelins, clubs, slings, axes with short handles, and two-handed axes with long handles. They brought with them paintings of the deeds they had performed in the service of the Sun and of the Incas, and also great drums and trumpets, with many musicians to play them. In short, they all came in the best attire they could manage and attended the festival in grandeur.

For three days previously, there was a general fast, and no fire was lighted in the houses. Even all men were restricted from sleeping with their wives. After the fast, in the evening before the festival, the sacrificial Inca Priests prepared the sheep and lambs for sacrifice, and also got readied, other offerings of food and drink that were to be offered to the Sun. All these offerings had been provided by people who came to the feast, not only the nobles and envoys, but also all their relatives and servants.

The Virgins of the Sun were engaged, during the night, in preparing an immense quantity of maize pudding called Canca. This was made up into small round cakes, about the size of an apple. The flour for this bread, especially for what was intended for the Inca king and those of the royal blood, was ground by the chosen virgins of the Sun, who cooked all the other food for this feast; that it might appear to be given rather by the Sun to his children than by his sons to him; and it was therefore prepared by the virgins, as women of the Sun.

Another huge number of women ground the corn and cooked the food for the common people. And though the bread was intended for the people, it was yet prepared with care, because this bread was looked upon as sacred, and was only allowed to be eaten once during the year, on occasion of this feast, which was, among the people, the festival of their festivals.

When the appointed day arrived, the Inca king and his court, followed by the whole population of the city, while marched according to their age and dignity. They assembled in the great square, at early dawn, to greet the rising of the Sun. Here they waited for sunrise, all of them being barefooted, and all watching the east with great attention. They all eagerly watched the arrival of their god and as soon as the his first yellow rays fell on the tops of the high temples of the capital, a shout of greetings broke forth from the assembled common people, accompanied by songs of triumph, getting louder and louder as his bright orb, rose above the mountain range towards the east. Hereafter, they worshipped, and kissed the air.

After these usual ceremonies, the King rose to his feet and offered a huge golden vessel to the Sun god. This vessel was filled with superior liquor made from maize. After that the ruler himself tasted it. He performed this ceremony as the first-born, in the name of his father, the Sun, and, with the cup in his right hand, invited all his relations to drink and then ordered to distribute it among his fellow noble men. Having given the invitation to drink, the king emptied the vessel into a jar of gold, which was dedicated to the Sun. Whence the liquor flowed down a stone from the great square to the temple of the Sun, thus being looked upon as drunk by the deity.

When this ceremony was also completed, all people who had gathered there, walked in a procession along with their king to the temple of the Sun. At two hundred paces before reaching the doors, all took off their shoes, but the King remained with his shoes on until he came to the doors. The Inca king and his relations then entered the temple as children of the god, and there worshipped the image of the Sun. The king offered to the Sun the golden vases with which he had performed the ceremony, and the other members of his family gave their cups to the Inca priests, who were set apart for that office. Having offered up the cups of the royal people, the priests came to the doors to receive those of the nobles, who took their places according to their seniority and presented the gold and silver articles that they had brought from their provinces as offerings to the Sun. These offerings were in the form of sheep, lambs, lizards, toads, serpents, foxes, tigers, lions, and many sorts of birds, in short, of all the animals in the provinces, each imitated from nature in gold and silver, though the size of each article was not big enough.

As soon as these offerings were made, the chiefs returned to their places in procession; and presently the priests came out with many lambs, llamas, and rams of all colours. All this flock was the property of the Sun. They took a black llama, for among the Indians this colour was preferred for the sacrifices, as more sacred. For they said that a black beast was black all over, while a white one, though its body might be white, always had a black nose, which was a defect, and caused it to be less perfect than a black beast. This first sacrifice of a black llama was made to judge the omens of the festival. For they almost always sacrificed a llama before undertaking any act either of peace or war, in order to see, by examining the heart and lungs, whether it was acceptable to the Sun, so as to say, whether it would be successful or not. In order to seek an omen to tell them whether a harvest would be good; for some crops they used a llama, for others a ram; but they never killed a fruitful sheep even to eat, until it was unable to bear any lamb.

The procedure followed for knowing the omen through sacrifice was that they took a lamb or sheep, and placed it with head towards the east. They did not tie its feet, but three or four Indians held it, and it was cut open on the left side while still alive. They then forced their hands in, and pulled out the heart with the lungs and gullet up to the mouth, and the whole had to be taken out entire, without being cut.

If the lungs were found palpitating, the omen was looked upon as most fortunate. If this omen appeared, they took no note of others that might appear of an opposite character. For they said that the excellence of this lucky omen would overcome the evil of all contrary signs. They then took the entrails, blew air into them, and fastened up the mouth, or held it tight with their hands. Presently they began to watch the ways by which the air entered and distended the veins and arteries. If they were very full of air, it was again looked upon as a good omen.

While on the other hand, if the beast rose to its feet while being cut open, in spite of those who held it; or if the entrails broke and did not come out whole. It was also an evil sign if the lungs or heart were torn or bruised in being pulled out. Returning to the details of the Raymi festival, if the sacrifice of the lamb did not furnish good results, they made another sacrifice of a sheep, and if its results were also found unsatisfactory, they offered up another. But, even if the third sacrifice was unlucky, they did not desist from celebrating the festival, though they did so with inward sorrow, believing that their father, the Sun, was enraged against them for some fault or negligence, that they must have unintentionally committed against his service. They feared that cruel battles, draught, diseases in their flocks, and other misfortunes might befall them. But when the omens were auspicious, their joy was very great with which they celebrated the festival, as they looked forward to the good fortune ahead.

After the sacrifice of the lamb, they brought a great quantity of lambs and sheep for a general sacrifice, and they did not cut these open while they were alive, but beheaded them first. The blood and hearts of all these, as well as of the first lamb, were preserved and offered to the Sun, and the bodies were burnt until they were converted to ashes.

It was necessary that the fire for the sacrifice should be new, and given by the hand of the Sun, as they expressed it. For this purpose they took a large bracelet, this was held by the high priest. It was larger than usual, and had on it a highly polished concave plate. They put this towards the Sun, at an angle, so that the reflected rays concentrated on one point, where they had placed a little cotton and the sunlight focused on one point soon lighted it. On this fire, thus obtained from the hands of the Sun, they offered all the sacrifices, and roasted all the meat on that day. Portions of fire were then conveyed to the temple of the Sun, and to the convent of virgins, where they were kept in for whole year. It was the duty of these virgins to keep the fire burning and it was considered to be an evil omen if they ever got extinguished. All the meat for the feast was roasted in public, in the two squares, and it was distributed among all those who were present at the feast, whether the royal Incas, the nobles or the common people. And each received a piece of bread with the meat. This was the first dish in their grand and solemn banquet. Afterwards they received a great quantity of eatables, which were eaten without drinking; for it was the universal custom of the Incas of Peru, not to drink while eating. After the eating was over, they brought liquor in great quantity.

The Inca king, seated in his golden chair, which was placed on a platform of the same metal, sent to the members of the tribes desiring them to drink, in his name, with the most distinguished Incas belonging to other nations. First, they invited the captains who had shown valour in war. Next the king ordered the nobles living in the vicinity of Cuzco, to be invited to drink. These chiefs, owing to the great privilege of bearing the name of Inca, which that Prince had granted them, were looked upon as nobles of the highest rank next to the Incas of the royal blood.

During these drinking sessions that the Incas had with each other, they all held their cups touching each other, two and two, and whether large or small, they were always of the same size and shape, and of the same metal, whether gold, silver or wood. This custom was enforced that each might drink the same quantity. He who gave an invitation to drink carried the two cups in his hands, and if the invited person was of lower rank he was given the cup in the left hand, if of equal or higher rank, the cup in the right; and with more or less ceremony according to the position in life of one and the other. Then they both drank together, and, the person inviting to drink, having received back his cup, returned to his place. On these occasions the first invitation was from a superior to his inferior, as a token of favour and kindness. Afterwards the inferior invited his superior, as an acknowledgment of his generousness and duty.

In observing this custom, the Inca king first sent an invitation to his nobles, in each nation preferring the captains before those who were not warriors. The Inca who took the invitation said to the invited person, "The sole Inca sends me to invite you to drink, and I come to drink with you in his name." The invited captain or noble or knight then took the cup with much reverence, raised his eyes to the Sun, as though giving thanks for such an undeserved favour conferred by his son, and having drunk, he returned the cup to the Inca without another word, only making signs of adoration with his hands and kissing the air with his lips.

And it should be noted that the Inca king did not send invitations to drink to all the nobles but only to some selected ones, who were most worthy and who were most devoted to the public good. The rest of the nobles were invited to drink by the same Inca nobles who had brought their cups back, but in their own names and not in that of the Inca king, which satisfied them, because the invitation came from one who was a child of the Sun, like their king.

After the first invitation to drink, the captains and nobles returned their greetings in the same order as they had received them; some of them returned to the Inca king himself, and the others to his relations. The Inca king was approached without a word, and merely with the signs of adoration. He received them with much pleasure, and took the cups they presented, but he did not rather could not drink all of them so he merely put his lips on them, drinking from some more, from others less, according to the favour he wished to show to the owners of the cups, which was regulated by their rank and merit. And he ordered the Inca attendants to drink for him with other captains and nobles. The nobles held these cups as a sacred thing, because the son of the Sun god, their Inca king had touched them with his hands and lips. They never drank out of them again, nor touched them, but looked upon them as idols to be worshipped, in memory of their having been touched by the king.

After the inviting and drinking session, all the people returned to their places. Then there was time for recreation by dancing and singing in different fashions and dresses used by each participating nation. While the singing and dancing continued no one left off drinking with the Incas, the captains and the nobles inviting each other, according to their special friendships, or to the neighbourhood.

This celebration at the feast of Raymi lasted for nine days, during which there used to be an abundance of eating and drinking, and such rejoicing as each person could show. But the sacrifices for observing omens were only made on the first day. As soon as the nine days were over, the nobles returned to their lands after taking the permission to do so from their beloved Inca king in a very joyful and contented spirit at having celebrated the principal feast of their god the Sun. If ever the Inca king was busy with war or in visiting his dominions, he celebrated the feast in the place where he happened to be while the Inca governor, the High Priest, and others of the royal blood who remained behind, took care to celebrate it in the capital. In such situations, the nobles assembled in their provinces, with each one going to the feast that was held nearest to the place of his abode.

Daily Life

Another part of Inca religious life was divination. Every important thing was undertaken with a consultation to divination. It was used to diagnose illness, to predict the outcome of battles, and even to judge for crimes, thus giving it a judiciary function. Divination was also used to determine what sacrifice should be made to what god. All this was done by consulting the oracles or after analysing the omens. Such a purpose was solved by, observing in a dish the meandering of a spider, or the disposition of cocoa leaves, by drinking ayahuasca, a narcotic that had profound effects on the central nervous system. This was believed to enable one to communicate with the supernatural powers. While, another common method was by examining the markings on the lungs of a sacrificed llama. The lungs were inflated by blowing into the dissected trachea and, after minutely observing the veins, the priests told future. And it was only after a positive reading that the decision of a political or military action was taken. Life was believed to be controlled by the unseen powers of the universe, and to determine these portents the priests had to communicate with the supernatural. Oracles were indeed considered to be the most important and direct means of direct access to the gods. A Spanish traveller has described one oracle of a huaca close to the Huaca-Chaca Bridge, across the Apurimac River near Cuzco, a wooden beam as thick as a fat man, with a girdle of gold about it with two large golden breasts like a woman. These and other idols were blood stained by the regular animal and human sacrifices. 'Through this large idol,' a chronicler wrote, 'the demon of the river used to speak to them.' Therefore it is clear that omens formed an important part of everyday life of the Incas from the common man to the Inca king.

Polygamy was also practiced among the Inca nobles as the king himself but common people were more happily contented with one wife only. This might be because of the lack of assets and food to feed so many wives. The marriage was conducted in a manner that gave it quite as original a character as compared to the other institutions of the country whether religious or social. On an appointed day of the year, all those of a marriageable age were called together in the great squares of their respective towns and villages, throughout the empire. The king appeared in person over the assembly of his own kindred, and taking the hands of the different couples, declared them as husband and wife. No one was allowed to select a wife beyond the community to which he belonged. After that a dwelling was made for the newly married pair at the cost of the administration, and the prescribed portion of the land was granted to them for their maintenance. The law of the Incas provided for the future, as well as for the present. It left nothing to chance. This simple ceremony of marriage was followed by common festivities among the friends of the parties, which lasted several days; as every wedding took place on the same day.

Deities

It is true that from the beginning of their empire the Incas were not always steadfast in their religion, nor maintained the same opinions and worshipped the same gods. Actually, at various times they took on many new rites and ceremonies in contact with the beliefs of the other communities that they had won from time to time, and though they eliminated some, they always kept loading the people down with more of them. It was in the name of religion that they made their conquests, with a thought that Viracocha, as the creator of the world, and the Sun, Thunder, and the rest of their gods must be honoured and obeyed properly. The Incas considered that their gods were responsible for preserving all creation by means of the power that was given by the gods to the Incas for this purpose. And as such they believed that their war was for a holy purpose.

Although it is true that the Inca kings required all conquered persons to follow their Inca religion, but those people were not required to abandon their natal religion totally. This was because the Incas only made the newly conquered subjects give up that part of their religion that seemed to contradict with the Inca religion. Therefore, not only the conquered people kept on worshipping their former gods, but the Incas themselves accepted these gods and brought their idols to their capital, Cuzco, where they were placed among the Incas' own gods. The Incas worshiped these new gods somewhat, but much less than they worshiped their own native gods.

But when any province rebelled against them, the Incas ordered the protective native gods of the rebellious province were to be brought out and put in public, where they were whipped carelessly every day until such province was made to serve the Incas again. After the rebels surrendered, their gods were restored to their places and honoured with sacrifices. At this time the Incas would say that the province had been subdued through the power of the rebels' gods, who wanted to avoid being insulted. And it was even said that the majority of the rebels surrendered just because they heard that the idols of their deities were exposed to public insults. This was also a field where religion was used for a purpose of winning the enemy.

The creator god of the Inca people was Viracocha, who was also recognized as a culture hero. The titles assigned to his greatness were numerous as the Creator of earth, man, and animals, Lord Instructor of the World, the Ancient One, and the Old Man of the Sky. Viracocha also went through several transformations simultaneously transforming the world around him in the course of time. He made people, destroyed them, and re-created them of stone; and when they were re-created, he dispersed mankind in four directions. As a culture hero he taught people various techniques and skills. He journeyed widely until he came to the shores of the present-day Ecuador in South America, where he set off into the Pacific, with either a boat made of his cloak, or as the others say that he walked on the water.

While Inti, the sun god, was indeed the highest ranked deity of the Incas. His warmth embraced the Andean earth and matured crops; and as such he was beloved by the farmers. Inti was represented with a human face on a golden disk. He was considered to be the divine ancestor of the Inca: "my father" was a title given to Inti by one Inca ruler.

Apu Illapu, the rain giver god, was an agricultural deity to whom the common man addressed his prayers for rain. Temples to Illapu were usually on high structures and in times of drought, pilgrimages were made to them and prayers were accompanied by sacrifices both animal and human, depending on the severity of the situation. The people believed that Illapu's shadow was in the Milky Way, from where he drew the water that he poured down as rain.

Mama-Kilya, wife of the sun god, was the Moon Mother, and the regulator of women's menstrual cycles. Silver was considered to be tears of the moon. The stars had minor functions. The constellation of Lyra, which was believed to have the appearance of a llama, was entreated for protection. The constellation Scorpio was believed to have the shape of a cat, the Pleiades were called "little mothers," and festivals were celebrated on their reappearance in the sky. Earth was called Paca-Mama, or 'Earth Mother.' The sea, which was relatively remote to the Inca until after 1450, was called Mama Qoca, the Sea Mother.

The Incas had already begun thinking of finding the explanations for the existence of each thing and causes for their origin. Later, they came to understand many of the second causes, which could be seen by their effects. Actually, they made a big mistake by believing that there was only one Universal Creator of all things, one god to whom they always made their prayers and sacrifices, while at the same time worshiping, with equal reverence and with the same ceremonial services other natural powers such as the sun, water, earth, and many other things that they considered divine. In each case they believed that these things had the power to make or preserve what was necessary for human life, and this was always their main interest. For this same reason, Incas felt that the other powers of nature should be worshipped equally as the Creator, and thus an infinite number of idolatries and superstitions were born and began affecting the daily lives of the common Inca people.

Actually they showed deep devotion, and each person was utterly careful to worship and sacrifice with all that he was assigned. The religion was so firmly established, universally accepted, and amazingly strict that they offered and sacrificed even their own children by killing them and their own property by burning it, as was their custom.

The most notable aspect of this religion is that they had nothing written down to learn, recite and keep. For that purpose, they memorized everything so exactly that it seemed as if these things were carved into the Incan bones. For this purpose alone, the Incas had more than a thousand men in the city of Cuzco who did nothing but remembered these things. Along with these men, other young boys were raised and these youngsters were so trained that these things would not be forgotten. Another important cult was practised in the name of Pachama, the mother of the earth.

As the religious life of the Incas was so developed, there was felt a need of a calendar for keeping account of the festivals. Thus the period of waxing and the waning moon was used to calculate monthly cycles, from which the time periods for Inca festivals were set. The 30-day calendar was religious, and each month had its own festival. But so little is known about the calendar used by the Inca that one can hardly make a statement about it for which a contrary opinion cannot be found. Some workers in the field even assert that there was no formal calendar but only a simple count of lunar days. Since there was no written language used by the Inca, it is impossible to check contradictory statements made by early colonial chroniclers. It is widely believed that the quipus of the Inca contain notations of the days, but no satisfactory demonstration of this is possible. Most historians agree that the Inca had a calendar based on the observation of both the Sun and the Moon, and their relationship to the stars. Names of 12 lunar months are recorded, as well as their association with festivities of the agricultural cycle; but there is no suggestion of the widespread use of a numerical system for counting time, although a decimal system, with names of numbers at least up to 10,000, was used for other purposes. The organization of work on the basis of six weeks of nine days suggests the further possibility of a count by triads that could result in a formal month of 30 days.

The descendants of the Inca are the present-day Quechua-speaking peasants of the Andes, who still constitute perhaps 45 percent of the population of Peru. They combine farming and herding with simple traditional technology. Rural settlements are of three kinds: families living in the midst of their fields, true village communities with fields outside of the inhabited centres, and a combination of these two patterns. Towns are centres of mixed-blood population. An Indian community is close-knit, with the member families usually intermarrying. Much of the agricultural work is done cooperatively. Their present day religion is a kind of Roman Catholicism infused with the pagan hierarchy of spirits and deities.

The Incas also kept records of their dynasties. For this purpose, they had a developed a very unique method. As they knew no script so they knotted onto the threads that were called 'quipu'. This was done with the help of professional accountants. The major local ethnic lords also kept records. Through the study of such quipu, modern researchers have learned that there was both a quantitative and a historical dimension to Andean records. One of the quipu refers to more than 20 separate events, all recorded in perfect historical sequence, but the way in which these events were recorded has not been understood yet. The quantitative record, which was easier to understand, lists the number of men and women on the first two cords, followed by the number of domestic animals llamas. Cloth, the most valuable commodity among the Incas comes first among the goods listed, followed by food and household items.

Religion was the basis of all the administrative procedures, but though the religion entered so largely and deeply into the conduct of the common people, their political institutions, their mythology, their cultural values, which were said to explain the natural phenomenon in full extent and the mysteries of the universe in full grandeur, was to the utmost limit mean. Their ideas in respect to a life after death drew more attention as they considered the existence of soul as true. They also believed that the body is resurrected after death. They also believed that there are two different and separate places assigned for the good and the wicked people. This was one of the earliest concepts of Heaven and Hell. The good people were imagined to pass a happy life in the sky, full of all the luxuries of life. While the wicked were punished by a long time of hard work at the centre of the earth and that was indeed the description of hell.

They believed that after death, the two souls that inhabit each person would take different ways. One would return to its place of origin - that actually depended upon the virtues of the dead, on the kind of death one had, as well as on the dead person's social and economical condition. The other soul remained in the body that was preserved intact and mummified. It is most probably this belief that led the Incas to bury personal belongings with the dead. As they believed that the occupations in the future world had great resemblance to those of the present, they buried their people of status and respect with some dresses that he had used in his life, his utensils and often his treasures too. Beside all this, they sacrificed his wives, favourite concubines and loyal servants for his company and for serving him in the abode of the sky. The dead bodies were mummified in an erect position, but more often in the sitting posture.

The Incas even built a vast network of roads throughout their empire. It comprised two north-south roads, one running along the coast for about 3,600 km, the other inland along the Andes for a comparable distance, with many interconnecting links. Many short rock tunnels and suspension bridges made of ropes of a human thigh thickness were also constructed. Use of the system was strictly limited to government and military business; a well-organized relay service carried messages in the form of knotted cords at a rate of 240 km a day. And it is a pity that this same network greatly facilitated the Spanish in their conquest of the Inca Empire and brought their end much earlier than it would have been through the natural process of civilization.

So we can see that under the Incan administration, there was the genius of government, that far from limiting itself to matters of public concern, penetrated into the most private fields of domestic life, allowing no man, however humble, to act for himself, even in those personal matters in which none but himself, or his family at most, might be supposed to be interested. No Peruvian was too low for the government and none was so high that he was not made to feel his dependence upon it in every act of his life. His very existence as an individual was absorbed in that of the community. His hopes and his fears, his joys and his sorrows, the tender sympathies of his nature; were all regulated by law. He was not allowed even to be happy in his own way he had to share it with every one in the community. The government of the Incas was the mildest, but the most idealistic and totally based on religion.

The Inca empire, constituted of numerous independent and even hostile tribes, yet, under the influence of a common religion, common language, and common government, they were knit together as one nation, animated by a spirit of love for its religion and institutions and devoted loyalty to its sovereign.

****

CHAPTER-2

AZTEC

Much before the advent of Europeans, the countries of Central America were already flourishing with highly cultured and developed social system present among the common people. The social system mainly comprised of different classes. This class system had found its roots in materialistic development of society through the ages. Therefore, the religions of Central America were also the result of an independent growth of the human mind under the effect of the surroundings and day-to-day life. These religions imaged true materialistic and social approaches of the common mass.

The Spanish imperialists were the first to destroy the cultural growth and loot the treasure of belief of these unmatched civilizations. During imperialistic advances, many Spanish travellers journeyed through remote areas of the sub-continent. They studied and found that the existing culture was of much different belief and advancement as compared to the contemporary European one. According to the travel accounts of different Spanish travellers, the agricultural development of the people of Central America was much advanced than the other people of the American continent. Almost everywhere, the agriculture was dependant on an artificial, man-made irrigation system. Workmanship was very intelligently divided among the people of the society and there were different sites where beautiful pottery was made. They even used alloys to make different things for the household and for battle purpose. Many were devoted for developing new skills in designing jewellery, knitting, etc. The inter-state business had also reached its height. On the basis of this, the social life became complex and the class system was followed strictly than ever.

But despite this fact, in all those religions, one thing was found common and that was the mixing of ancient form of tribal religion with the religious beliefs of the conquerors. The most advanced among them was the religion of the Aztecs, which flourished over a wide region of the present day Mexico in Central America.

The Azteca or Aztecs were a nomad tribe of doubtful origin, probably of Nahua blood. While wandering over the Mexican plateau for generations, they at length settled in the marshlands near the Lake of Tezcuco. The name Azteca means 'Crane People.' They were named so because of the fact that, like cranes, they dwelt in a marshy neighbourhood. This people on their arrival in Mexico were in a very inferior state of culture, and were probably little better than savages. Later, they founded the town of Tenochtitlan (Mexico) and became the most powerful allies, whom they finally surpassed entirely in power and splendour. And after they conquered pre-existing tribes, the religion of the locals was totally affected by them and thus a simple agriculture based religion turned highly complex with the practice of human sacrifice.

The features of the Aztecs as represented in various Mexican paintings are typically Indian. The race was of an average height, and the skin slightly dark brown in complexion. In a general outlook, these people were grave and melancholic, with a deeply rooted love of the mysterious, slow to anger, yet almost inhuman in the violence if passions were aroused. They were gifted with a logical mind and a quickness of apprehension. They had a real affection for the beautiful in nature and a passion for flowers, but the Aztec music lacked joy, and the national amusements were too often of a gloomy character.

Legend of the Foundation of the capital city

The most popular legend tells that the nomadic Nahua people beheld perched upon a cactus plant an eagle of great size and majesty, grasping in its talons a huge serpent, and spreading its wings to catch the rays of the rising sun. The soothsayers or medicine-men of the tribe, reading a good omen in the spectacle, advised the leaders of the tribe to gather listening to the voice of what they considered divine authority, they proceeded to drive piles into the marshy ground, and thus laid the foundation of the great city of Mexico.

A lively elaboration of this legend tells us how the Aztecs had sought refuge upon the western shore of the Lake of Tezcuco, in an island among the marshes on which they found a stone on which one of their priests had sacrificed a prisoner prince, some years ago. A noble plant (cactus) had sprung from there and upon this a royal eagle sat grasping the serpent in his talons. Beholding in this a good omen, and urged by a supernatural impulse which could not be explained, a priest of high rank jumped into a nearby pool and found himself face to face with Tlaloc, the god of waters. After an interview with the deity the priest obtained permission from him to found a city on the site, from the humble beginnings of which arose the metropolis of Mexico (Tenochtitlan).

The city was so planned that four great roadways built at right angles to one another it intersected it. As the city was situated in the middle of a lake, it was traversed by numerous canals, which were also used as passages through the city. The four principal ways met at its shores. The dwellings of the poorer classes were chiefly composed of adobes, but those of the nobility were built of a red porous stone that was quarried close by. They were usually of one story only, but were spread on a larger piece of ground and had flat roofs, many of which were covered with flowers. In general they were coated with hard, white cement, which gave them an added resemblance to the Oriental type of building.

A little apart from the common dwellings and the market places, the temples rose high. These were not actual temples but high step pyramids of stone around which a staircase led to the summit, on which was usually erected a small shrine containing the idol of the deity. A kind of gatehouse on each side gave access to the enclosure. The mass of this structure was composed of a mixture of rubble, clay, and earth, covered with carefully worked stone slabs, cemented together with infinite care, and coated with a hard gypsum.

The prayers and rituals were performed in a large number of temples, which were built in a shape that resembled the step-pyramids of Egypt but with a difference that their tops ended in a big and open platform.

The principal complex of worship of Huitzilopochtli was surrounded by forty such inferior temples and shrines. In this were collected the relics of the countless victims who had been sacrificed to the war-god of the Aztecs, and in this horrid structure the Spanish conquerors, at the time of conquest, counted no less than 136,000 human skulls.

Social and Religious Structure

As agriculture was the main source of livelihood, whole social structure revolved round it. The religion of the people of Mexico was also based on the agricultural beliefs and rituals of the pre-Aztec community. It was practiced with the worship of the guardian gods of agriculture, special secret rituals for rain and also considering corn as a heavenly thing.

But later, these ancient beliefs came under the effect of the developed religious concept of the ruling Aztecs. The social and administrative structure of the Aztecs turned complex. The class system was present and the society was classified into nobles, independent community members, knights, servants and other tax paying communities. The priests were treated as a special class, who had cut themselves from the social and economic life and had devoted themselves to purely religious acts. They knew to calculate time and were also appointed as teachers to the nobles and future priests. All the priests followed strict discipline and were kept under restrictions of various types.

Aztecs beliefs were based in their perception of nature, its time space, and cycles. They were particularly concerned with the destructive aspect of nature, and most of their rituals are means of avoiding the destructive and chaotic forces of nature, and finding harmony within nature.

Deities and their legends

The heavenly and worshipped circle of the Aztecs was quite large and well defined. Many of gods were considered as a symbol of natural powers and many were associated with different trades. But the most important and powerful among them were the gods related to agriculture and cultivation. The name of Tlaloc is to be mentioned in first place as the 'god of rain'. Among others were Centeotl, the god of maize harvest and a goddess related to fertility and childbirth.

Tlaloc, the Rain God

Tlaloc was the god of rain and moisture. And in an old country such as of the Aztecs, where the harvest depended entirely upon rainfall, he was a deity of high importance. It was believed that he dwelt in the mountains that surrounded the valley of Mexico, as these were the source of the local rainfall. In Aztec idols, he is generally represented in a semi-recumbent attitude, with the upper part of the body raised upon the elbows, and the knees half drawn up, probably to represent the mountainous character of the country that was responsible for rainfall. He was married to Chalchihuitlicue, who bore him numerous issues in the form of clouds. Many of the figures that represented him were carved from the green Jade stone, to depict the colour of water, and in some of these he was shown holding a serpent of gold to show his power in the form of lightning. Tlaloc manifested himself in three forms, as the lightning-flash, the thunderbolt, and the thunder. Although his image faced the east, where he was supposed to have originated but he was worshipped as being the inhabitant of the four cardinal points and even every mountaintop. The colours of all the four elements, yellow, green, red, and blue, were used to image his costume, which was further crossed with streaks of silver, symbolising mountain torrents. Even a vase containing grain was usually placed before his idol as an offering of the growth. He dwelt in a many-watered paradise called Tlalocan (The Country of Tlaloc), a place of plenty and fruitfulness, where those who had been drowned or struck by lightning or had died from dropsy enjoyed eternal bliss.

Many maidens and children were sacrificed to Tlaloc on the eve of his annual festivals. If the children wept it was regarded as a happy omen for a rainy season. The festival of Etzalqualiztli was held on a day approximating to May 13, about which date the rainy season usually commenced in the region. Another festival in his honour was Quauitleua, commenced on the start of the Aztec year on February 2. At the former festival the priests of Tlaloc plunged into a lake, imitating the sounds and movements of frogs, which, as denizens of water, were under the special protection of the god. Chalchihuitlicue, his wife, was often symbolised by the small image of a frog.

The Maize-Gods

There was a group of deities, called Centeotl that had a significant effect on the agriculture and the farmers of the Aztec empire. Each one of these deities personified one or other aspect of the maize-plant. The chief goddess of maize was Chicomecohuatl (translation: Seven-serpent), her name being an allusion to the fertilising power of water. She symbolised the green ear of the maize. Although it is possible that she was a pre-Nahua deity and was accepted by the Nahua tribe as 'Mother Earth'. This goddess also had a son, Centeotl, a male maize-spirit. Her spring festival was held annually on April 5 and was called

Hueytozoztli. This festival was celebrated by a general fast, with the dwellings of the Aztec people decorated with bulrushes that had been sprinkled with blood drawn from the extremities of the inmates. The worshippers then proceeded to the maize-fields, where they pulled the tender stalks of the growing maize, and, having decorated them with flowers, placed them in the common storehouse. The girls of the village presented the goddess with bundles of maize of the previous season's harvesting, later restoring them to the granaries in order to utilise them for seed for the coming year. Chicomecohuatl was always represented among the household deities of the Mexicans, and on the occasion of her festival the family placed before her image a basket of provisions surmounted by a cooked frog, bearing on its back a piece of cornstalk stuffed with pounded maize and vegetables. This frog was symbolic of Chalchihuitlicue, wife of Tlaloç, the rain-god, who assisted Chicomecohuatl in providing a bountiful harvest. In order that the soil might benefit, a frog, the symbol of water, was sacrificed, so that its vitality should help the weary earth to gain fertility.

Quetzalcoatl

Other than these, the highest level of importance was given to three gods of different origin. The first one among them was Quetzalcoatl who was an ancient god with all the mystery and power of totemic. It is quite possible that Quetzalcoatl was a deity of the pre-Nahua people of Mexico. He was regarded by the Aztec race as a god of alien character, and had a limited number of followers in Mexico. He was later imaged as an old man with a long white beard. The city of Cholula was the centre of his worship.

It was here that the biggest temple, related to him was situated. He was regarded as 'The Father of the Toltecs,' and, legend says, was the seventh and youngest son of the Toltec king, Iztacmixcohuatl. The word Quetzalcoatl literally means 'Feathered Serpent,' became a ruler of Tollan, and by his encouragement of the liberal arts he helped in the advancement and development of his people. Later, his exile brought peculiar changes in the country. He buried his treasures of gold and silver, burned his palaces, and banished all the birds from the neighbourhood of Tollan. He proceeded to Tabasco, the fabled land of Tlapallan, and, embarking upon a raft made of serpents, floated away to the east. Another legend says that the king cast himself upon a funeral pyre and was consumed, and that the arising ashes flew upward and was changed into brilliant birds. His heart also soared into the sky, and became the morning star. The Mexicans believed that when he died he was invisible for four days, and that for eight days he wandered in the underworld, after that when he achieved resurrection, he appeared as the morning star and ascended his throne as a god. Another more probable explanation of his origin is that which would regard him as the Man of the Sun, who has quitted his abode for a season for the purpose of teaching mankind those arts that represent the first steps in civilisation. Quetzalcoatl was represented as a traveller with staff in hand, and this is proof of his solar character, as is the statement that under his rule the fruits of the earth flourished more abundantly than at any subsequent period. Gold was accumulated in abundance during his reign and as this metal is associated with the sun so this assists his origin from the sun. In the native pinturas it is noticeable that the solar disc and semidisc are almost invariably found in connection with the feathered serpent as the symbolical attributes of Quetzalcoatl.

The titles bestowed upon Quetzalcoatl by the Nahua people show that in his solar significance he was god of the heavens, as well as merely son of the sun. He was also called by the name Ehecatl (translation: The Air), Yolcuat (translation: The Rattlesnake), Tohil (translation: The Rumbler), Nanihehecatl (translation: Lord of the Four Winds) and Tlauizcalpantecutli (translation: Lord of the Light of the Dawn).

Tezcatlipoca

The second one was Tezcatlipoca, who was related to the burning and destroying power of the sun. His symbol was a glass shield that pointed towards the circular shape of the sun and in which he was supposed to see reflected the actions and deeds of mankind. He was considered as a cruel god who always demanded sacrifice. Tezcatlipoca, often called the 'Fiery Mirror' was undoubtedly the Jupiter of the Nahua pantheon. The evolution of this god from the status of a spirit of wind or air to that of the supreme deity of the Aztec people is quite interesting. Tezcatlipoca naturally advanced so speedily in popularity and public honour that it was little wonder that within a comparatively short period he became the god of fate and fortune, and was inseparably connected with the national destinies and calamities.

Tezcatlipoca was intimately associated with the legends that account for the overthrow of Tollan, the capital of the Toltecs, the earlier inhabitants of the Mexico region. His chief adversary on the Toltec side is the god-king Quetzalcoatl, who was regarded as the enemy of Tezcatlipoca. The rivalry between these gods symbolised that which existed between the civilised Toltecs and the barbarian Nahua. There is also a popular legend that explains it well. It is said that in the days of Quetzalcoatl there was abundance of everything that was necessary for survival. The maize was plentiful and cotton grew in all colours without having to be dyed. A variety of birds sang sweet songs all day long and gold, silver, and precious stones were in abundance. In a few words it can be said that in the reign of Quetzalcoatl there was peace and plenty for all men.

But this blissful state did not continue for long. Envious of the calm enjoyment of the god and his Toltecs people, three wicked men plotted their downfall. This refers to the gods of the invading Nahua tribes, the deities Huitzilopochtli, Titlacahuan or Tezcatlipoca, and Tlacahuepan. These laid evil enchantments upon the city of Tollan, and Tezcatlipoca in particular took the lead in these envious conspiracies. Disguised as an aged man with white hair, he presented himself at the palace of Quetzalcoatl, where he said to the attendants, "Present me to your master, the king, I desire to speak with him."

The servants advised him to retire, as Quetzalcoatl was indisposed and could see no one. He requested them, however, to tell the god that he was waiting outside. They did so, and he was summoned in.

On entering the chamber of Quetzalcoatl, the witty Tezcatlipoca said in a sympathetic tone, "How are you, my son? I have brought you a drug which you should drink, and which will put an end to the course of your malady."

"You are welcome, old man," replied Quetzalcoatl.

I have known for many days that you would come. I am exceedingly indisposed. The malady affects my entire system, and I can use neither my hands nor feet."

Tezcatlipoca assured him that if he had the medicine that he had brought, he would immediately experience a great improvement in health. Quetzalcoatl drank it and at once felt much revived. The cunning Tezcatlipoca gave him another cup and still another cup and as it was nothing but the country wine he speedily became intoxicated, and submitted to his will.

Soon, Tezcatlipoca, in pursuance of his inimical policy, took the form of an Indian went to the palace of Uemac, who was the chief of the Toltecs in temporal matters. This person had a fair and beautiful daughter who was desired in marriage by many of the Toltecs. This princess, on seeing Tezcatlipoca in the disguise of an Indian, fell deeply in love with him, and her passion was so intense that she became seriously ill because of her longing for him. The chief Uemac, hearing this went to see her and inquired the cause of her illness. He was told the truth. Listening this, he immediately ordered the arrest of Tezcatlipoca. Later when Tezcatlipoca was brought to his court. The conversation between both of them started as such.

"Where have you come from?" inquired Uemac.

"Lord, I am a stranger, and I have come to these parts to sell green paint," replied Tezcatlipoca.

"Why are you dressed in this fashion? Why don't you wear a cloak?" asked the chief.

"My lord, I follow the custume of my country," replied Tezcatlipoca.

"You have inspired love in the heart of my daughter," said Uemac. "What should be done to you for thus disgracing me?"

"Kill me; I care not," said the cunning Tezcatlipoca.

"No," replied Uemac, "for if I kill you my daughter will die. Go to her and say that she may wed you and be happy."

Now this marriage of Tezcatlipoca, to the daughter of Uemac aroused much discontent among the Toltecs. In order to divert their attention, Uemac made a war on the neighbouring state of Coatepec. The Toltecs army assembled and having arrived at the country of the men of Coatepec they placed Tezcatlipoca in fierce battle with his bodyguards, hoping that he would be slain by them. But Tezcatlipoca and his men killed a large number of the enemy and compelled them to flee. The chief Uemac celebrated his triumph warmly. The knightly honours were placed upon his head, and his body was painted with red and yellow which was an honour reserved for those who distinguished themselves in the battlefield.

Tezcatlipoca announced a great feast in Tollan, where all the people from far and near were invited. On the drumbeat, the crowd danced and sang in the city. Tezcatlipoca sang to them and forced them to accompany the rhythm of his song with their feet. Faster and faster the people danced, until the pace became so furious that they were driven to madness, lost their balance, and tumbled down to a deep ravine, where they were changed into rocks. Others who attempted to cross a stone bridge drowned in the water below, and were changed into stones.

The Toltecs were so worried by the advancements of Tezcatlipoca that it was soon apparent to them that their fortunes were on stake and that the end of their empire was at hand. Quetzalcoatl, their king, was so moved at the turn of the situation that he decided to quit Tollan and go to the countryside from where he had come on his civilising mission to Mexico. Having once decided that, he burnt all the houses which he had built, and buried his treasure of gold and precious stones in the deep valleys between the mountains. He changed the cocoa trees and even ordered all the singing birds to quit the valley and follow him to a distance of more than a hundred leagues. On the way to his destination, he discovered a big tree at a point called Quauhtitlan. He had a rest there and asked his attendants to bring a mirror. When the mirror was brought, he exclaimed at his own image, "I am old," and from that circumstance the spot was named Huehuequauhtitlan that means 'Old Quauhtitlan'. While being accompanied by his musicians he walked and walked towards his destination until he was tired. Then he sat on a rock and left his hand imprints on that. Later, at another place named Coaapan, he met the inimical Nahua gods.

"Where do you go? He was asked, "Why do you wish to your capital?"

"I am going to Tlapallan," replied Quetzalcoatl, " from where I came."

"For what reason?" He was asked.

"My father the Sun has called me there," replied Quetzalcoatl.

"Go, then, happily," they said, "but leave us the secret of your art, the secret of founding in silver, of working in precious stones and woods, of painting, and of feather-working, and other matters."

But Quetzalcoatl refused, and cast all his treasures into the fountain of Cozcaapa (Water of Precious Stones). At Cochtan, he met another enchanter, who on learning his destination granted him a draught of wine. On tasting it, Quetzalcoatl was overcome with sleep. Continuing his journey in the morning, the god passed between a volcano and the Mountain of Snow, where all his attendants died of cold. He regretted this misfortune exceedingly, and wept, lamenting their fate with most bitter tears and mournful songs. But on reaching the summit of the mountain, he slid to the base. Then, arriving at the seashore, he made a raft of serpents, and was drifted by the waves towards the land of Tlapallan.

So we can see that in the Aztec mythology, Tezcatlipoca was much more than a mere personification of the wind, and if he was regarded as a life-giver he also had the power of destroying existence. In fact on occasions he appears as a death-dealer, and as such was called Nezahualpilli (The Hungry Chief) and Yaotzin (The Enemy). Perhaps one of the names by which he was best known was Telpochtli (The Youthful Warrior), from the fact that his reserve of' strength, his vital force, never diminished, and that his youthful and boisterous vigour was apparent even in the tempest.

The Aztecs pictured Tezcatlipoca as the wind of night rushing along the deserted roads with more fierce fullness than the day itself. Indeed one of his names, Yoalli Ehecatl, signifies 'Night Wind.' Even benches of stone were set along the highways for his special use, that on these he might rest after his fierce, horrifying and splendid journey. These seats were concealed by green boughs, beneath which the god was supposed to wait for his victims. But if one of the persons he seized overcame him in the struggle he might ask for whatever boon he desired.

It was supposed that Tezcatlipoca had guided the Nahua tribe, and especially the people of Tezcuco, to the valley of Mexico. But he was not a mere local deity of Tezcuco; his worship was being widely celebrated throughout the country. His exalted position in the Mexican pantheon won him special reverence as a god of fate and fortune. His priestly caste far surpassed the status of other Aztec gods. All the gods were worshipped for some special purpose, but the worship of Tezcatlipoca was regarded as compulsory, and to some extent as a safeguard against the destruction of the universe.

The Spanish writers of the 16th century have described a very grand ceremonial festival that was celebrated to please their god Tezcatlipoca. This was the biggest social and religious event of the spring season.

Huitzilopochtli

The third one was Huitzilopochtli. He was an ancient figure related to the bird totems. But despite his relation with such small creatures, he was considered to be very cruel and blood thirsty god. He was said to be demanding sacrifices all the time. He was later given the regard of being the god of war and as such he gained an important position in the Heavenly circle of the Aztecs. His place in the pantheon was similar to that of Mars in the Roman. Human sacrifices were performed to please him. For this purpose the captives and the young men from the families of the nobles were chosen. The Aztecs fought war from time to time not for treasures, not for the extension of the land but only for their religious cause – getting captives for sacrifice.

The legend of his origin says that, under the shadow of the mountain of Coatepec, near the city of Tollan, there lived a pious widow called Coatlicue who had a daughter named Coyolxauhqui. Everyday she went to the small hill in order to pray to the gods. One day, during her prayers, she saw a small colourful ball falling over her. She was pleased by the bright colours and placed it in her bosom, intending to offer it up to the sun god. Some time afterwards she learnt that she was to become the mother of another child. Her sons, hearing of this, abused her humiliating her in every possible way. Coatlicue went about in fear and anxiety; but the spirit of her unborn infant came and spoke to her and consoled her. Her sons decide to kill her because of the defamation she had brought to their race.

Having decided that for once, they dressed themselves in their war attire. But one of them named Quauitlicac and said in reference to the still unborn Huitzilopochtli, who had replied to him: "O brother, listen attentively to what I have to say to you. I am fully informed of what is about to happen." But with the intention of slaying their mother, they went in search of her while Coyolxauhqui was leading their group. Quauitlicac climbed the mountain to acquaint Huitzilopochtli with the news that his brothers were approaching to kill their mother.

"Look out where they are," replied the infant god. "To what place have they advanced?"

"To Tzompantitlan," responded Quauitlicac.

Later on Huitzilopochtli asked: "Where are they to be found now?"

"At Coaxalco", was the reply.

Huitzilopochtli asked again to what point his enemies had advanced.

"They are now at Petlac," Quauitlicac replied.

After a little while Quauitlicac informed Huitzilopochtli that they were at hand under the leadership of Coyolxauhqui. At the moment of the enemy's arrival Huitzilopochtli was born, along with a shield and spear of a blue colour. He was painted, his head was surmounted by panache, and his left leg was covered with feathers. He shattered Coyolxauhqui with a flash of serpentine lightning, and then he chased the others, whom he pursued four times round the mountain. They did not attempt to defend themselves, but fled. Many perished in the waters of the adjoining lake, to which they had rushed in their despair.

The name Huitzilopochtli signifies 'Humming-bird'. He was called so because he wore the feathers of the humming-bird on his left leg. Huitzilopochtli's image is seen surrounded by serpents, with him resting on serpent-shaped supporters. His sceptre was a single snake, and his great drum was of serpent-skin.

In American mythology the serpent is closely associated with the bird. Thus the name of the god Quetzalcoatl is translatable as "Feathered Serpent," and similarly Huitzilopochtli is regarded as a god the primary conception from whom the idea of the serpent, the symbol of warlike wisdom and might, the symbol of the warrior's dart or spear, and the humming-bird, the harbinger of summer, type of the season when the snake or lightning god has power over the crops arose.

Huitzilopochtli was usually represented as wearing a waving panache or plume of hummingbirds' feathers on his head. His face and limbs were striped with bars of blue, and in his right hand he carried four spears. His left hand bore his shield. The shield was made with reeds, covered with eagle's feathers. The spear was also tipped with tufts of soft feather instead of flint. These weapons were placed in the hands of those who as captives engaged in the sacrificial fight, for in the Aztec mind Hultzilopochtli symbolised the warrior's death. Huitzilopochtli indeed was the war-god of the Aztecs, and was supposed to have led them to the site of Mexico from their original home in the north. The city of Mexico took its name from one of its districts, which was designated by a title of Huitzilopochtli's, Mexitli (translation: Hare of the Aloes).

But Huitzilopochtli was not a war-god alone. As the serpent-god of lightning he had a connection with summer too, the season of lightning, and therefore to some had dominion over the crops and fruits of the earth. The Nahua believed that Huitzilopochtli could grant them fair weather for the fructification of their crops, and they placed an image of Tlaloc, the rain-god, near him, so that, if necessary, the war-god could compel the rainmaker to exert his blessings to guard them from floods. So, if war was not waged annually the gods could not be offered sacrifices and if the gods succumbed the crops would fail, and famine would destroy the race. So it was small wonder that Huitzilopochtli was one of the chief war-gods of Mexico.

Huitzilopochtli's principal festival was the Toxcatl, celebrated immediately after the Toxcatl festival of Tezcatlipoca, to which it bore a strong resemblance. Festivals of this god were held in May and December. It was in December that his image was moulded in dough and kneaded with the blood of sacrificed children. Then this image was pierced by the priest with an arrow that signified of the death of Huitzilopochtli until his resurrection in the next year.

Strangely enough, when the absolute supremacy of Tezcatlipoca is remembered, the high priest of Huitzilopochtli, the Mexicatl Teohuatzin, was considered to be the religious head of the Mexican priesthood. The priests of Huitzilopochtli held office by the right of descent.

Some other deities:

Food-Gods

To the Aztec community, the most important deities were the food-gods. When Nahua tribe in course of progress, emerged from the hunting to the agricultural state of living, they became totally dependent on the harvest from earth. The Aztecs soon became aware of the fact that the old deities could not avail them in the same manner as the guardians of the crops and fertilisers of the soil. So, with the advance of power, even the terrible war-god had an agricultural significance. A distinct bargain with food-gods could be seen clearly and included mutual assistance as well as provision for mere alimentary supply. In no mythology is the understanding between god and man so clearly defined as in the Nahuan, and in none other, a better example could be found.

Xipe

Xipe (translation: The Flayed) was widely worshipped throughout the Aztec empire. At his special festival, the skins were removed from the victims and captives and were worn by devotees of the god for succeeding twenty days. In mythology, he was usually represented as of a red colour. In later days of Aztec monarchy, the kings and leaders of Mexico assumed the attire of this deity Xipe. This dress consisted of a crown made of feathers, a jacket of feathers, and an apron of green feathers lapping over one another in a tile-like pattern. Xipe also held a shield in his hand. This shield was a round target covered with the rose-coloured feathers, with concentric circles of a darker hue on the surface. He was imagined as possessing three forms, the first that of the roseate spoon bill, the second that of the blue coating, and the last that of a tiger, the three shapes perhaps corresponded to the regions of heaven, earth, and hell, or to the three elements, fire, earth, and water.

Nanaliuatl, or Nanauatzin

Nanahuatl (translation: Poor Leper) presided over skin diseases, such as leprosy. It was thought that persons afflicted with these complaints were set apart by the moon for his service. In Nahua tongue the words for 'leprous' and 'eczematous' also mean 'divine.' Legend says that before the sun was created humanity dwelt in sable and horrid gloom. Only a human sacrifice could hasten the appearance of the luminary. Metztli (The Moon) led forth Nanahuatl as a sacrifice, and he was cast upon a funeral pyre, in the flames of which he was consumed. Metztli also cast herself upon the mass of flame, and with her death the sun rose above the horizon. There can be no doubt that the myth refers to the consuming of the starry or spotted night, and incidentally to the nightly death of the moon at the flaming hour of dawn.

Xolotl

Xolotl is of southern origin. He represents either fire rushing down from the heavens or light flaming upward. He was imaged as sitting opposite to the picture of the setting sun being devoured by the earth. He is probably identical with Nanahuatl, and appears as the representative of human sacrifice. He has also some resemblance with Xipe. On the whole Xolotl may be best described as a sun god of the more southerly tribes. Xolotl was a mythical figure quite foreign to the Aztec people, who regarded him as something strange and monstrous. He was imaged with empty eye-sockets. Legend says that when the gods determined to sacrifice themselves in order to give life and strength to the newly created sun, Xolotl withdrew, and wept so much that his eyes fell out of their sockets.

The Fire-God

To the Aztecs, this deity was known by various names, notably Tata (translation: Our Father), Huehueteotl (translation: Oldest of Gods), and Xiuhtecutli (translation: Lord of the Year). He was imaged in the colour of fire, with a black face, a headdress of green feathers, and bearing on his back a yellow serpent, just to typify the serpentine nature of fire. He also bore a mirror of gold to show his connection with the sun. On rising in the morning all Mexican families made Xiuhtecutli an offering of a piece of bread and a drink. He was thus not only the god of thunderbolts, but also the milder deity of domestic hearth. Once in a year, fire in every Mexican house was extinguished, and rekindled by friction before the idol of Xiuhtecutli. When a Mexican baby was born it passed through a baptism of fire that had been burning since its birth on the fourth day, to nourish its existence.

Mictlan

The full name of this deity was Mictlantecutli (translation: Lord of Hades). He was the 'God of the Dead' and shadowy realm to which the souls of men repair after their mortal end. He is represented as a grisly monster with capacious mouth, into which all the spirits of the dead fell. His terrible abode was sometimes indicated as Tlalxicco (translation: Navel of the Earth), but the Aztec people believed that it was situated in the far north, which they regarded as a place of famine, desolation, and death. It was here that the people who were unfit to enter the paradise of Tlaloc, those who had not been drowned or had not died a warrior's death, passed a meaningless existence. In his images, he is seen surrounded by a species of demons, and had a wife who was named Mictecaciuatl.

Worship of the Planet Venus

In Aztec mythology, planet Venus is called as Citlalpol (translation: The Great Star) and Tlauizcalpantecutli (translation: Lord of the Dawn). It was indeed the only star worshipped by them. Upon its rising they stopped up the chimneys of their houses, so that no harm of any kind might enter with its light. There was a column called Ilhuicatlan (translation: In the Sky) that stood in the court of the great temple of Mexico, and upon this a symbol of the planet was painted. On its reappearance during its usual circuit, captives were taken before this representation and sacrificed to it. It was represented as the lord of the ninth division of thirteen days. He is imaged as having a white body with long red stripes, while round his eyes was a deep black painting like a domino mask, bordered with small white circles. His lips were bright. The black paint on the face, surrounding the eye, typifies the dark sky of night. In Mexican and Central American symbolism the eye often represents light, and here, surrounded by blackness as it is, it is perhaps almost hieroglyphic. As the star of evening, Tlauizcalpantecutli was some times represented with the face of a skull, to signify his descent into the underworld, where he followed the sun.

Elements of Sun Worship

The Nahua people regarded the sun as the supreme deity, the principal source of existence and life. His worship served as a background to the worship of all the other gods. In Aztec mythology, he was named lpalnemohuani (translation: He by whom Men Live) shows that the Mexicans regarded him as the primary source of being, and the heart, the symbol of life, was looked upon as his special sacrifice. Those who rose at sunrise to prepare food for the day held up the hearts of animals they had slain for cooking, and even the hearts of the victims to Tezcatlipoca and Huitzilopochtli were first held up to the sun, as if he had a primary right to the sacrifice. It was supposed that the luminary rejoiced in offerings of blood, and that it constituted the only food that was supposed to provide him that extra energy to undertake his daily journey through the heavens. He was often imaged licking up the gore of the sacrificial victims with his long tongue-like rays. The Mexicans believed that eternity had been broken up into epochs, marked by the destruction of successive suns. In the earlier period too, a mighty deluge had deprived the sun of life, and similar things happened at the end of every 'sheaf' of fifty-two years. The old suns were dead, and the current sun was no more immortal than they. So they thought that at the end of one of the 'sheaves' he too would succumb.

Therefore they thought it necessary sustain the sun by the daily food of human sacrifice because they believed that only with a human sacrifice he would be satisfied. This could be most suitably found among the inhabitants of a neighbouring state. It thus became the business of warrior class in the Aztec state to furnish forth the altars of the gods with human victims. Various communities in the region, despite the fact that they had been related earlier had begun to regard each other as traditional enemies, and on a given day in the year their forces met at an appointed spot for the purpose of engaging in a battle which should furnish one side or the other with a sufficiency of victims for the purpose of sacrifice. The warrior who captured the largest number of opponents alive was regarded as the champion of the day, and was awarded the chief honours of the combat. The sun was therefore the god of warriors, as he would give them victory in battle in order that they might supply him with food of human sacrifice. On March 17 and December 1 and 2, at the ceremonies known as Nauhollin (translation: The

Four Motions-alluding to the quivering appearance of the sun's rays), the warriors gathered in a hall for the purpose of despatching a messenger to their lord the sun. High up on the wall of the principal court was a great symbolic representation of the orb, painted upon with bright coloured hanging cotton. Before this other gums and spices were burned four times a day. The victim, a war-captive, was placed at the foot of a long staircase leading up to the Quauhxicalli (translation: Cup of the Eagles), the name of the stone on which he was to be sacrificed. He was clothed in red striped with white and wore white plumes in his hair-colours symbolical of the sun, while he bore a staff decorated with feathers and a shield covered with tufts of cotton. He was then addressed by the officiating priest in the following terms: "Sir, we pray you go to our god the sun, and greet him on our behalf; tell him that his sons and warriors and chiefs and those who remain here beg of him to remember them and to favour them from that place where he is, and to receive this small offering which we send him. Give him this staff to help him on his journey, and this shield for his defence, and all the rest that you have in this bundle." The victim, having once undertaken to carry the message to the sun god, was then sacrificed and thus despatched upon his long journey. The Mexican warriors believed that they continued in the service of the sun even after their death. They believed that after death they were admitted to the dwelling of the god and shared all the delights. The Mexican warrior dreaded to die in his bed, and craved for an end on the battlefield. They believed that they would partake of the cannibal feasts that were offered daily to the sun and including the juice of flowers.

Totec

Totec (translation: Our great chief) was a solar deity who had been adopted from the people of an alien state and therefore he was not regarded as the principal sun god. His festival was celebrated by the symbolical slaughter of all other gods for the purpose of providing sustenance to the sun, each of the gods being figuratively sacrificed in the person of a victim. Totec was imaged in attire that resembled that of an Aztec warrior. His festival was a seasonal one, as only bunches of dried maize were offered to him. But its larger and symbolic meaning was obvious. It was a commemoration of the creation of the sun. Totec was the only deity of the Aztecs who directly represented the sun. As a borrowed god he would have but a minor position in the Mexican pantheon, but again as the only sun god whom it was necessary to bring into prominence during a strictly solar festival he would be for the time a very important deity.

Tepeyollotl or Tepeolotlec

The word Tepeyollotl means 'Heart of the Mountain', and represents a deity whom the Nahua connected with seismic disturbances and earthquakes. His name referred to the condition of the earth after flood. The sacrifices of his thirteen days were not good, and the literal translation of their name is 'dirt sacrifices.' These days were celebrated with a feast to the Jaguar, and the last four preceding days were the days of fasting. Tepeolotlec also means the 'Lord of Beasts.' The Aztecs believed that this Tepeolotlec was the same as the echo of the voice when it re-echoes in a valley from one mountain to another. This name 'jaguar' is given to the earth because the jaguar is the boldest animal, and the echo that the voice awakens in the mountains is a survival of the flood.

From this we can see that Tepeyollotl was a deity of the pure and simple earth, a god of desert places. It is certain that he was not a Mexican god, or at least was not of Nahua origin.

Macuilxochitl, or Xochipilli

Macuilxochitl (translation: Five-Flower and Source of Flowers) was a deity who was considered as the patron of luck in gaming. The worship of this god was very widespread. There was a festival held in his honour, which was preceded by a rigorous fast. The people covered themselves with ornaments and jewels symbolic of the deity, as if they desired to represent him, and dancing and singing proceeded happily to the sound of the drum. Offerings of the blood of various animals along with delicious cakes were offered to the god. This simple fare was later followed by human sacrifices, rendered by the notables, who brought certain of their slaves for immolation.

Father and Mother Gods

The Aztecs believed that Ometecutli and Omeciuatl were the father and mother of the whole human species. Their names signified the Lords of Duality or Lords of the Two Sexes. They were also called as Tonacatecutli and Tonacaciuatl (translation: Lord and Lady of Our Flesh). They were regarded as the sexual essence of the creative deity and they occupied the first place in the Nahua calendar, and thus symbolised that they had existed from the beginning. They were imaged as being clothed in rich attire. Ometecutli (translation: Two-Lord) was sometimes identified with the sky and the fire-god, while the female deity Omeciuatl represented the earth or water-conceptions.

The Pulque-Gods

The liquor that the Aztecs drank was called 'pulque' and was made from the juice of Agave Americana. When a person was intoxicated after having been drunk, he was believed to be under the influence of a god or spirit. The commonest form under which the drink-god was worshipped was the rabbit. This particular deity was also known as Ometochtli. The chief pulque-gods apart from these were Patecatl and Tequechmecauiani. If the drunkard desired to escape the perils of accidental hanging during intoxication, it was necessary to sacrifice to them. If the drinker wished his punishment not to exceed a headache, Quatlapanqui (translation: The Head-splitter) was sacrificed to, or else Papaztac (translation: The Nerveless) was offered the sacrifices. The calendar day of Ometochtli was under the special protection of these gods, and the Mexicans believed that any one born on that day was almost inevitably doomed to become a drunkard. All the pulque-gods were closely associated with the soil, and with the earth-goddess. They wore a golden nose-ornament of a crescent shape. This ornament was also inscribed upon all articles that were considered sacred to the pulque-gods. Their faces were painted red and black, as were objects consecrated to them, including their blankets and shields. These drink-gods were of the same class as the food-gods of the fruitful soil.

The Goddesses Metztli

Metztli, or Yohualticitl (translation: The Lady of Night), was the Mexican goddess of the moon. She in reality had two types of images common among the people. On one hand, she was considered as a beneficent protector of harvests and promoter of growth in general, and on the other she was considered as the cause of dampness, cold, and miasmic airs ghosts, mysterious shapes of the dim half-light of night and its silence.

To any person in the agricultural stage of civilisation the moon appears to be a great recorder of harvests. But she also had supremacy over water, which is always connected by with the moon. Citatli (Moon) and Atl (Water) are constantly confounded in Nahua myth, and in many ways their characteristics were blended.

Tlazolteotl

It was the earth goddess who was named Tlazolteotl (translation: Goddess of Ordure), by the Nahua people. She was also called Tlaelquani (translation: Filth-eater) because she was considered the eradicator of sins. People went to confess their sins to the priests who remained in her service. On one hand, Tlazolteotl was the goddess of confession while on the other; she was also considered as the goddess of desire and luxury.

For confessing his sins, a person visited the priest who acquainted the applicant with the day that appeared the most suitable for his confession, according to the calendar. When the awaited day arrived, the person provided himself with a mat, copal gum to burn as incense, and wood to burn it. If he was a person holding a high office, the priest went to his house, but in the case of common people the confession took place in the dwelling of the priest. After having lit the fire and burned the incense, the penitent addressed the fire in the following terms: "O lord! You are the father and mother of the gods, and the most ancient of them all, see that your servant, your slave bows before you. Weeping and bearing pains, he approaches you in great distress. He comes plunged in grief, because he has been buried in sin and has enjoyed evil delights which merit death. O master most compassionate, you are the upholder and defence of all, receive the penitence and anguish of your humble slave."

This prayer having concluded, the confessor then turned to the person and addressed him as such: "My son, you have come into the presence of that god who is the protector and upholder of all; you have come to him to confess your evil vices and your hidden dirt of soul; you have come to him to reveal the secrets of your heart. Take care that you omit nothing from the catalogue of your sins in the presence of our lord who is called Tezcatlipoca. It is certain that you are before him who is invisible and impalpable, you who are not worthy to be seen before him, or to speak with him" These allusions to Tezcatlipoca were to him in the shape of Tlazolteotl. Having listened to a sermon by the confessor, the person then confessed his misdeeds, after which the confessor said: "My son, you have confessed your evil deeds before our lord god. I wish to say in his name that an obligation is to be made by you during the celebration of the feast of the goddesses of carnal things. You shall fast for four days, punishing your stomach and your mouth. That day you shall also scarify your tongue with the small thorns and if that is not sufficient you shall do the same to your ears. You will have to pierce a spine in your tongue and then you shall scarify your shoulders. Having done that, the sins will be pardoned."

Chalchihuitlicue

Chalchihuitlicue was the wife of Tlaloc, the god of rain and moisture. The translation of the word Chalchihuitlicue means 'Lady of the Emerald Robe'. She was specially worshipped by the water-carriers of Mexico. Her costume was bit peculiar as round her neck she wore a wonderful collar of precious stones, from which a gold pendant hung. Her image was seen crowned with a coronet of blue paper, decorated with green feathers. While her eyebrows were of turquoise, set in as mosaic, and her garment was of a nebulous blue-green hue, as if reminding of the tint of seawater in the tropics. This resemblance was even highlighted by a border of sea-flowers or water-plants, one of which she also carried in her left hand, while in her right she bore a vase surmounted by a cross which symbolised the four points of the compass from where rain came.

Mixcoatl

Mixcoatl was the Aztec god of the chase. His name could be translated as 'Cloud Serpent', and this originated the idea that Mixcoatl was a representation of the tropical whirlwind. Like many other gods of the chase, he is figured as having the characteristics of a deer or a rabbit. He was seen imaged as carrying a sheaf of arrows, to typify thunderbolts.

Ixtlilton

Ixtlilton (translation: The Little Black One) was the Mexican god of medicine and healing, and therefore was also known as the brother of Macuilxochitl, the god of well being or good luck. His painted images on the walls of the ancient temples reveal that he would have emerged from the status of a primitive Shaman.

It was a well-practised tradition that the parents of children who benefited from the treatment bestowed a feast on the deity, whose idol was carried to the residence of the grateful father, where ceremonial dances and offerings were made before it. It was then thought that Ixtlilton descended to the courtyard to open fresh jars of pulque liquor provided for the feasters, and the entertainment concluded by an examination by the Aztec of such of the pulque jars dedicated to his service. If these were found unclean, it was understood that the master of the house was a man of evil life. Then the priest presented him with a mask to hide his face from his fellow friends.

Omacatl

Omacatl held the status of the god of festivity and joy. His namc could be literally translated as 'Two Reeds'. Rich people of the community worshipped him. They organised splendid feasts in his name. His idol was placed in the chamber where these functions were to take place, and the Aztecs considered it an offence if there was any omission in the prescribed procedure of worship. It was believed, if such a thing happened the deity might appear by himself and rebuke the host of the feast. It was even believed that the deity might no longer regard the host as his devotee and might abandon him. And after that a falling-sickness, might seize the guests too.

Such beliefs led the people to form a great bone out of maize paste, pretending that it was one of the bones of the deity whose merry rites they were about to engage in, this was done prior to the feast. Then they washed it down with large quantities of pulque. The idol of Omacatl was provided with a small space in the region of its abdomen, and into this the offered provisions were stuffed. He was represented as a figure that was painted black and white, crowned with a paper coronet, and hung with coloured paper.

Opochtli

Opochtli (translation: The Left-handed) was the god considered sacred to the fishers and bird-catchers. As we know that in early time, the Aztecs were marsh dwellers. And these marsh dwellers had been dependant on fish and birds for their daily food. So it is possible that this god had been a newer and reformed image of some earlier deity. In their mythology, the Aztecs credited this god with the invention of the harpoon for spearing fish and the fishing rod and bird-net.

The fishermen and bird-catchers of Mexico were so grateful to this god that they held a special feast in honour of him, at which certain liquor called octli was consumed. After that a procession was formed, in which the old people who had dedicated themselves to the worship of the god, marched. Opochtli was represented, as a man painted black with his head decorated with the plumes of native wild birds, and crowned by a paper coronet in the shape of a rose. He was clad in green paper that fell to the knee, and he wore white sandals. In his left hand he held a red shield with a white flower at the centre. This flower had four petals that were placed crosswise. While in his right hand he held a sceptre in the form of a cup.

Yacatecutli

Yacatecutli was a god who was considered the patron of travellers of the merchant class. These people worshipped him by piling together their staves on which they sprinkled blood from their noses and ears. The traveller's staff symbolised this deity. The people said their prayers to this very symbol and offered flowers and incense.

MAJOR FESTIVALS AND SACRIFICES

The Teotleco Festival

The supreme position occupied by Tezcatlipoca in Mexican religion and his authority over the people is well exemplified in the following details of the festival of the Teotleco. The word Teotleco can be translated as 'Coming of the Gods.'

The scriptures and chronicles speak of this festival in great grandeur. It is said that this festival was celebrated in the twelfth month of the Aztec calendar. It is said that this festival was to honour all the deities who had gone to some other country for the time being. On the fifteenth day of this month, young boys decked all the altars of gods with boughs. This work was paid for in maize. Some received a basketful, and others only a few ears. Then on the eighteenth day, the ever-youthful god Tlamatzincatl or Titlacahuan arrived. It was said that he marched better and arrived first because he was strong and young. Food was offered him in his temple on that night. Every one drank, ate, and enjoyed. Old people especially celebrated the arrival of god by drinking wine, and it was alleged that his feet were washed by these rejoicings. Finally, on the last day of the month, celebrations of this festival reached its epoch, as it was believed that all the gods had returned. On the preceding night a quantity of flour was kneaded on a carpet into the shape of a cheese, because it was supposed that gods would leave a footprint thereon as a sign of their return. The chief attendant watched all night, going to and fro to see if the impression appeared. When he at last saw it he called out, 'The master has arrived,' and at once the priests of the temple began to sound horns, trumpets, and other musical instruments used by them. Upon hearing this noise every one set forth to offer food in all the temples. Next day the aged gods were supposed to arrive, and young men disguised as monsters were put into a huge sacrificial fire.

The Toxcatl Festival

This was another important festival related to Tezcatlipoca, the god with the greatest destructive power. This was held in the fifth month of the Aztec calendar. On the day of festival a youth was slain who for an entire year previously had been carefully instructed. He was selected from among the best war captives of the year, and was without any blemish. He bore the name and attributes of Tezcatlipoca himself. He was seen upon with regard and awe by the whole Aztec community. He was even imagined to be the representative of Tezcatlipoca on this earth.

He rested during the day, and walked out of the palace at night, armed with the dart and shield of the god. This practice was symbolical of the wind-god's progress over the highways and crossroads at night. He carried a special whistle along with and blow it producing the sound that resembled the howling of the wind at night. Small bells were attached to his legs and arms that rang with his every movement. He had some attendants always following him and at intervals, he rested on the stone seats built on the roadside for the convenience of Tezcatlipoca.

Later in the year he was mated to four beautiful maidens of high birth, with whom he passed his time in luxury and amusement of every description. He was entertained at the tables of the nobility as an earthly representative of Tezcatlipoca, and his latter days were one constant round of feasting and excitement. At last on the fatal day of the festival, the captive had to pay for all the pleasures and luxuries with the price of his life. He took a tearful farewell of the maidens and was carried to the temple for sacrifice. When he reached the summit he was received by a high priest, who let him lie on the stone platform and cut his chest open taking out his heart.

Xalaquia Festival

This was a festival to please Chicomecohuatl, the Aztec goddess of maize. As food held so importance in the Nahua tribe, this goddess was also considered to be a very important one. Her blessings were always sought. The festival of Xalaquia, which lasted from June 28 to July 14, commenced exactly when the maize plant had attained its full growth.

At that time the village women let their hair loose and shook and tossed it so that by sympathetic magic the maize might take the hint and grow correspondingly long. The maize liquor and maize porridge was consumed in great quantities on that day. This was followed by night dances that were performed in temple premises. The central figure in such dances was a female captive or slave who was painted red and yellow in face to represent the colours of the maize-plant. She was named Xalaquia.

She had previously under gone a long course of training in the dancing-school, and now, all unaware of the horrible fate awaiting her, she danced happily among the rest. Throughout the duration of the festival she danced and on its expiring night she was accompanied in the dance by the women of the community, who circled round her, praising the goddess Chicomecohuatl for her deeds. At the time of sunrise, they were joined by the chiefs and headmen who; danced the solemn death-dance, along with the exhausted and half-fainting victim. The entire community then approached the pyramid of sacrifice and on reaching its summit, the victim was stripped to a nude condition, the priest plunged a knife of flint into her bosom, and, tearing out the still palpitating heart, offered it up to Chicomecohuatl. In this manner the goddess, weary with the labours of inducing growth in the maize-plant, was supposed to be refreshed. Hence the name Xalaquia, which signifies 'She who is clothed with the Sand.' Until the death of the victim it was not lawful to partake of the new corn.

The Offering to Centeotl

During her last hours the victim sacrificed at the Xalaquia wore a ritual dress made from the fibres of the aloe, and with this garment the maize-god Centeotl was later clothed. Having been dressed as such, he was temporarily represented as the earth-goddess, so that he might receive her sacrifice. The blood of victims was offered up to him in a vessel decorated with that brilliant and artistic feather work. Upon partaking of this blood offering the deity emitted an intense groan. This ceremony followed by the tasting of the soil, which consisted in raising a little earth on one finger to the mouth and eating it.

As has been said, Centeotl the son has been confounded with Centeotl the mother, who is in reality the earth mother-Teteoinnan. Each of these deities had a temple of his or her own, but they were closely allied as parent and child. But of the two, Centeotl the son was the more important. On the death of the sacrificed victim her skin was conveyed to the temple of Centeotl the son, and worn there in the succeeding ritual by the officiating priests. This gruesome dress is frequently depicted in the Aztec images, where the skin of the hands, and in some instances the feet, of the victims can be seen dangling from the wrists and ankles of the priest.

Sacrifices to Tlaloc

In the mountains of the Aztec empire, there were certain points where sacrifices were made to please Tlaloc. At certain places, there were artificial ponds to sacrifice humans. Offerings to the god were made near the common burial-place of bodies of the victims slain in his service. The statue of Tlaloc was placed on a mountain and at various points, five or six young children were annually offered to the god. Mountains were regarded as his special high places, and on the heights were built his temples, in which his image was found carved in green stone.

The Aztecs believed that due to the constant production of food and falling of the rain, the deities, who were responsible to provide them, grew tired. The Aztecs tried to avoid this situation because they feared that if they did not feed the gods, they might perish hence resulting to famine and disaster. So, they gave a period of rest and once in eight years a festival called the Atamalqualiztli (translation: Fast of Porridge-balls and Water) was held for the purpose. During this festival, every one in the Nahua community returned for the time being to the conditions of savage life. Dressed in costumes representing all forms of animal and bird life, the people danced round the temple of Tlaloc for the purpose of diverting and entertaining him after his labours in producing the fertilising rains of the past eight years. A lake was filled with water snakes and frogs, and into this people plunged, catching reptiles in their mouths and swallowing them alive. The only grain food that was used for eating purpose during this season of rest was thin water-porridge of maize.

If some rich peasant wanted a special rainfall for the growth of his crops he sought out one of the professional makers of dough or paste idols, whom he desired to mould one of Tlaloc. To this image offerings of maize-porridge and pulque were made. Throughout the night the farmer and his neighbours danced, shrieking and howling round the figure for the purpose of invoking Tlaloc from his drought bringing slumbers.

Sacrifices to Quetzalcoatl

The worship of Quetzalcoatl was done, by shedding blood of the worshipper by himself. The celebrant or devotee drew blood from the vessels lying under the tongue or behind the ear by drawing across those tender parts a cord made from the thorn-covered fibres of agaves. The blood was smeared over the mouths of the idols.

The Aztec Priesthood

The importance of priests is unquestionable in any ancient religion. The Aztec priesthood was a hierarchy in whose hands a good portion of power of the upper classes resided. The mere fact that its members possessed the power of selecting victims for sacrifice must have been sufficient to place them in a position of enormous power. Their prophetic utterances, interpreting omens, etc. proved to be a great feature in the life of the Aztec people But despite exercising so much power, the priesthood enjoyed no easy existence, but led a tough life of fasting, penance, and prayer, with constant observance of an exacting ritual, which embraced sacrifice, the upkeep of perpetual fires, the chanting of holy songs to the gods, dances, and the superintendence of ever recurring festivals. They were required to rise during the night to render praise, and to maintain them in a condition of absolute cleanliness. We have seen that blood offering was a common method of sacrifice, and in this the priests engaged personally on frequent occasions. Education was entirely conducted by priesthood. Education was, indeed, highly organised. It was divided into primary and secondary grades. The priests instructed boys while the holy women instructed girls. The secondary schools were called calmecac, and were devoted to the higher branches of education. The curriculum included the study of hieroglyphic script, astrology and divination, with a wealth of religious instruction.

The Dread of the Last Day

According to the Aztecs, a god named Tlocnahuac created the universe. The history of universe was considered as a sequence of different periods or ages one after another. They believed that till then four ages had already passed with each age ending with fire, flood, storm or draught destroying everything and thus bringing an end to the life on earth. So with the conclusion of each period of fifty-two years a terrible dread came upon the Mexicans that the world would come to an end.

As the first day of the fifty-third year dawned, people narrowly observed the Pleiades cluster near the Orion constellation. They believed that once the cluster crossed the zenith, the world might be saved. For the purpose, gods were refreshed by the slaughter of a human victim, on whose still living breast; a fire of wood was kindled by friction. This fire consumed the heart and body. As the planets of hope crossed the zenith loud acclamations resounded from the people. The domestic hearths, which had been left cold and dead, were rekindled from the sacred fire that had consumed the sacrifice. In their view, mankind was safe for another period of fifty-two years.

The calendar system was the source of all Mexican science, and regulated the recurrence of all religious rites and festivals. In fact, the entire mechanism of Aztec life was resident in its provisions. The Mexican year was a cycle of 365 days, without any other correction.

Concluding in short, it can be said that the religion of the ancient Mexicans was a polytheism or worship of a pantheon of deities, the general aspect of which presented similarities to the systems of ancient Greece and Egypt. A superficial examination of the Nahua religion might lead to the conclusion that entire mythology presents only the fantastic attitude of the barbarian mind towards different forces of nature. As a matter of fact, the Aztecs displayed a theological advancement greatly superior to that of the Greeks or Romans. At the time of Spanish conquest, the Aztec priesthood was advancing to the contemplation of the exaltation of one god, whose worship was fast excluding that of similar deities. Through the study of the contemporary Spanish chronicles, it is found that much of the Nahua ritual and many of the prayers were unquestionably genuine, and displayed the attainment of a high religious level.

****

CHAPTER-3

HOPI

The word Hopi has been derived from the word 'Hopitu,' which means 'peaceful ones,' or 'Hopitushinumu,' which means 'all peaceful people.' While in common language, the word 'Hopi' literally means the 'righteous people,' or the 'correct people.' This is their epithet that was common among the other Native Americans. They were called so because they had been most successful in preserving their traditions and culture in comparison to other communities, ancient and modern. These people had been living in the southwest part of the United States for generations. And to protect themselves from others, they built their homes high atop the rocky platforms where there they are protected on most sides by cliffs. It was in the summer of 1540, when Coronado sent his men to visit seven villages, in the province of Tusayan, toward the northwest and as such the Hopi first became known to white men. At first, the Spaniards were not received with friendliness, but the opposition of the natives was soon overcome and the party remained among the Hopi for several days. There the Spaniards learned about the existence of the Grand Canyon of the Colorado.

The next Spaniard to visit Hopi tribe was Juan de Onate who was the governor and colonizer of New Mexico. He had already took possession of the country and made the Indians swear obedience and vassalage to Spain on November 15th, 1598. Their spiritual welfare was assigned to Fray Juan de Claros, but no active missions were established among the Hopi till scores of years. The five villages at that particular time, as far as it is possible to determine them, were Aguato or Aguatuybá (Awatobi), Gaspe

(Gualpe Walpi), Comupaví or Xumupamí (Shongo povi), Majananí (Mishongnovi), and Olalla or Naybf (Oraibi).

Then the first actual missionary work undertaken among the Hopi was in 1629,when Francisco de Porras, Andres Gutierrez, Cristobal de la Concepcion, and Francisco de San Buenaventura, along with twelve soldiers, reached Awatobi, where the mission of San Bernardino was founded in honour of the day, followed by the establishment of missions also at Walpi, Shongopovi, Mishongnovi, and Oraibi. The natives of Awatobi later poisoned this priest Porras in 1633. But despite this incident, all the Hopi missions worked well until 1680, when in the general pueblo (pueblo is a cluster of stone dwellings, similar to a small village) revolt of that year four resident missionaries were killed and the churches were destroyed. Therefore no attempt was made to re-establish any of the missions except that of Awatobi in 1700. But this also raged anger in the Hopi community and they attacked it at night, killing many of its people and compelling its permanent abandonment.

Legend of Origin

As it is with every religion, the Hopis also have legends telling of the creation of world and life. It is said that a very long time ago, everything was covered with water. Water was seen everywhere and all around. Then, in the direction of the rising sun, Huruing Wuhti, the deity of all hard substances, lived in the ocean. Her house was like a hideen half underground chamber quite similar to the Hopis of the day. There was a skin of a gray fox and one of a yellow fox tied to the ladder that led the way into the chamber.

There was also another Huruing Wuhti who lived in the west of the ocean. She also dwelt in a similar chamber but with a difference that a turtle shell rattle was attached to the ladder. It is also said that the Sun also had existence at that time. Shortly before rising in the east the Sun dressed up in the skin of the gray fox and started the time of dawn which was often termed as the 'white dawn of the Hopi.' After a little while the sun lay off the gray skin and put on the yellow fox skin, and then came the bright dawn of the morning which was termed as the 'yellow dawn of the Hopi.' Then the sun rose and it was said that it emerged from an opening in the north end of the chamber in which Huruing Wuhti lived. When arriving in the west again, the sun first announced his arrival by fastening the rattle on the point of the ladder beam, from where he would enter the chamber, passing through an opening in the north end and as such continuing his course eastward under the water and so on.

So in the course of time, these two deities caused some dry land to appear that raised upwards from the water. The Sun passing over this dry land constantly took notice of the fact, that there were no living beings on it. He immediately mentioned this fact to the two deities. So Huruing Wuhti of the west sent a message through the Sun to the Huruing Wuhti of the east, calling her to discuss this problem. The Huruing Wuhti of the east agreed on the point and proceeded to the West through a rainbow. They both consulted each other about the situation and decided that they would create a little bird; so the deity of the east made a wren of clay, and covered it up with a piece of cloth. Then they sang a song over it, and after a little while the little bird showed signs of life. When they uncovered the cloth, a live bird came forth. On seeing it the deities said to it that they wanted it to fly all over the dry place and see whether it could find anything living on it. They thought that as the Sun always passed over the middle of the earth, he might have failed to notice any living beings that might exist in the north or the south. So the little bird flew all over the earth, but when it returned, it reported that no living being existed anywhere.

The deity of the west then proceeded to make many birds of different kinds and form, placing them again under the same cover under which the first bird had been brought, to life. They again sang a song over them. Presently the birds began to move under the cover. The goddess removed the cover and found under it all kinds of birds and fowls. Then the two deities taught every bird the sound that it should make, and then the birds scattered out in all directions.

Then the Huruing Wuhti of the west made different kinds of animals of clay, and they were brought to life in the same manner as the birds. They were also taught by their creators their different sounds or languages, after which they proceeded forth to inhabit the different parts of the earth. Now both the deities wished to create man. The deity of the east first made a woman of clay and then a man, who were brought to life in exactly the same manner as the birds and animals before them. They were told that they should live upon this earth and should understand everything. Then the Huruing Wuhti of the east made two tablets of some hard substance and drew certain characters upon them with the wooden stick. Then they handed these tablets to the newly created man and woman, who looked at them, but did not know what they meant. So the deity of the east rubbed with the palms of her hands, first the palms of the woman and then the palms of the man, by which they were enlightened so that they understood the writing on the tablets. Thus the deities taught these two a language.

After they had taught them the language, the goddess of the east took them out and led them over a rainbow, to her home in the east. They stayed there for four days, after which Huruing Wuhti told them to go and select a place for themselves and live there. The two proceeded forth saying that they would travel around a while and wherever they would find a good field they would remain. Finding a nice place at last, they built a small, simple house, similar to the old houses of the Hopi. Soon the Huruing Wuhti of the west began to think of the matter again and communicated her thoughts to the Huruing Wuhti of the east that something more had to be done.

Meanwhile a Spider Woman had heard about all this matter and she also decided to create some beings. So she also made a man and woman of clay, covered them up, sang over them, and brought to life her handiwork. But these two proved to be Spaniards. She taught them the Spanish language, also giving them similar tablets and imparting knowledge to them by rubbing their hands in the same manner as the woman of the East had done. After this, the Spider Woman continued to create people in the same manner as she had created the Spaniards, always a man and a woman, giving a different language to each pair. But all at once she found that she had forgotten to create a woman for a certain man, and that is the reason why now there are always some single men.

The Huruing Wuhti of the west called the goddess from the

east and told her that she was feeling lonely and so she wanted some good people to live there. Then she also created a number of other people, but who were always a man and a wife. They were created in the same manner as the deity of the east had created hers. They lived in the west. Only wherever the people that Spider Woman had created came in contact with these good people there was trouble.

The people at that time led a nomadic life, living mostly on meat. Wherever they found rabbits or deer they killed them and ate. This led to a good many contentions among the people. Finally the Woman of the west said to her people: "You remain here; I am going to live, after this, in the midst of the ocean in the west. When you want anything from me, you pray to me there." Her people regretted this very much, but she left them. The Huruing Wuhti of the east did exactly the same thing, and that is the reason why at the present day the places where these two live are never seen.

Those Hopi, who want something from them, now deposit their prayer offerings in the village. When, they make their wishes and say prayers, they think of those two who live in the far distance. But even today the Hopi believe that they still remember them. The people of the Spider woman (the Spanish) were angry on Huruing Wuhti and two of them took their guns and proceeded to the abiding place of the deity. The Spaniards were very skilled and they found a way to get there. When they arrived at the house of Huruing Wuhti she was aware of their evil intentions. She asked them to lay down their weapons. They laid down their arms. Then she went to the rear end of her dwelling and brought out a white lump like a stone and laid it before the two men, asking them to lift it up. One tried it, but could not lift it up, and what was worse, his hands stuck to the stone. The other man tried to assist him, but his hands also stuck to the stone, and thus they were both prisoners.

Then Huruing Wuhti took the two guns and rubbed them between her hands to powder. She then said to them they should live in peace with one another. She also said that the people of Spider Woman knew many things, and the people whom they both had made also knew many, but different, things. So, she asked them not to quarrel about those things, but learn from each other; if one had or knew a good thing he should exchange it with others for other good things that they knew and had. She even wished to release them if they agreed to do as said. The Spanish agreed instantly and promised that they would no more try to kill the deity. On being assured, the deity went to the rear end of the dwelling where she disappeared through an opening in the floor. From there she exerted a secret influence upon the stone and thus released the two men. They departed, but Huruing Wuhti did not fully trust them, thinking that they would return, but they never did.

Legend of the Hopi coming from the Under World

There is a legend common among the Hopi community that tells about the people coming up on the earth for living. The legend says that a long time ago the people lived below. There were a great many of them, but they often quarrelled with each other. Some of them abused the women and the maidens, and that was the cause of strife among the people. So the chiefs, who were worried and angry over this, had a council and concluded that they should try to find another place to live. So they first sent out a bird named Motsni, to find a place of exit from that under world. It flew up high but was too weak and returned without succeeding. They then sent the Mocking-bird called as Yahpa. It was strong and flew up very high and soon it found a place of exit. On returning, it reported this to the chiefs.

Meanwhile the chiefs had caused a great flood. Due to this, many serpents came out of the ground with the water, and a great number of people were killed. When the Mocking-bird reported to the chiefs, they immediately announced through the crier that in four days they would leave, and that the women should prepare some food, and after they had eaten on the fourth day they would all assemble at the place right under the opening which the Mocking-bird had found.

The chiefs then planted a pine-tree, sang around it, and by their singing they made it grow very fast. It grew up to the opening which the Yahpa bird had found, and when the chiefs tried and shook it, they found that it was fairly strong, but not strong enough for many people to climb up on, especially its branches, which were very thin. So they planted another kind of pine, sang around it, and also made it grow up fast. This tree and its branches was much stronger than the other, but while the first one had grown through the opening, this one did not reach it entirely, its uppermost branches and twigs spreading out sideways before they reached the opening. Then they planted a reed, which proved to be strong, and also grew through the opening like the first pine tree. Finally they planted a sunflower, and as it was moist where they planted it, it also grew up very fast and to a great size, its leaves also being very large; but the sunflower did not reach the opening. Its very large disk protruded downward before it reached the opening. The sunflower was covered with little thorns all over.

Then the Spider Woman and her brother, and the Mocking-bird that had found the opening, climbed up on the tree respectively. After they had emerged through the opening, she embraced the first pine tree, her brother the reed, both holding them firmly that they should not shake when the people were climbing up. The Mocking-bird sat close by and sang a great many songs. Spider Woman was also sitting close by watching the proceedings. Now the people began to climb up, some on the first pine tree, others on the second pine and still others on the reed. As soon as they emerged, the Mocking-bird assigned them their places and gave them their languages. To one it would say: "You shall be a Hopi, and that language you shall speak." To another: "You shall be a Navaho, and you shall speak that language." And to a third: "You shall be an Apache, a Mohave, a Mexican," etc., including the White Men.

In the under-world the people had been very bad, being many sorcerers and dangerous people, just like there are in the villages today who are put diseases on the people. The people kept on coming out, and before they were all out the songs of the Mocking-bird were exhausted. And at once the people who were still on the ladders commenced returning to the under-world, but a very great many had already come out, an equally large number having remained in the under-world. At this time no sun existed and it was dark everywhere. Then the chief threw the ball upward to a great height, all the people stood and watched. When it came down it fell upon the head of some one and was shattered. But as it happened this was the chief's nephew. He was considered to be a bad soul, so the chief asked him to return to the under world. But he refused and prayed before him to keep him in his company.

Then the chief consented and let his nephew remain. It was still dark, and as there was no sunshine it was also cold, and the people began to look for fire and for wood, but as it was so dark, they could find very little wood. They thus lived there for a while without fire, but all at once they saw a light at a distance and the chief said some one to go and see there. When they had still been in the lower world they had occasionally heard footsteps of some one up above. So some one went in search of the light, but before he had reached it he became tired and returned. Another was sent and he got there. He found a field in which corn, watermelons, beans, etc., were planted. All around this field a fire was burning, which was kept up by wood, and by which the ground was kept warm so that the plants could grow. The messenger found a very handsome man there. He had four strands of turquoise around his neck and very large turquoise ear pendants. In his face he had two black lines running from the upper part of his nose to his cheeks. By his side was standing his friend who looked very ugly, with large open eyeholes and a large mouth. So it was a Skeleton whom they had heard walking about from the other world. The Skeleton then fed the messenger with some of his good things that he had there. The people had not brought much food with them from below and so they had not very much left. The people were very glad for this invitation and went to the place where Skeleton lived. But when they saw the small field they thought that the food would perish soon. But Skeleton always planted and the food was never gone. When they came there they gathered some wood and built a fire and then they warmed themselves and were happy. Skeleton gave them roasting ears, and watermelons, melons, squashes, etc., and they ate and refreshed themselves. Some of the plants were very small yet, others still larger, so that they always had food.

So the people remained there, made fields, and they always kept up a fire near the fields, which warmed the ground so that they could raise a crop. When the crop had matured they gathered it all, and when they had provisions they planned to start off again, but there was still no sun, and it was cold. So the chiefs all met in council with Skeleton, and talked this matter over in order to see whether they could not make a sun as they had had it in the underworld, but they did not just know how to do it. So they finally took a piece of dressed buffalo hide, which they cut in a round shape, stretched it over a wooden ring, and then painted it with white paint. They then pulverized some black paint with which they drew a picture of the moon around the edge of this disk, sprinkling the centre of the disk with the same black colour. They then attached a stick to this disk. Hereupon they stretched a large piece of white native cloth on the floor and placed this disk on it. All these objects they had brought with them from the underworld.

They then selected some one and directed him to stand on this moon symbol. Then the chiefs took the cloth by it, corners, swung it back and forth and then threw it upward, where it continued swiftly flying eastward into the sky. So the people sat and watched. All at once they noticed that it became light in the east. Something was burning there as they thought. The light became brighter and brighter, and something came up in the east. It rose higher and higher, and where the people were it became lighter and lighter. So now they could go about and they were happy. That turned out to be the moon, and though it was light, the light was only dim and the people, while working in the fields, would still occasionally cut off their plants because they could not see things very distinctly. It was still cold and the people were freezing, and they still had to keep the ground warm with fires. So, the chiefs again met in council, and concluded that perhaps the buffalo skin was not good, and that it was too cold, so they decided that this time they would take a piece of native cloth. They again cut out a round piece, stretched it over a ring, but this time painted it with oxide of copper. They painted eyes and a mouth on the disk, and decorated the forehead of what this was to resemble in yellow, red, and other colours. They put a ring of cornhusks around it, which were worked in a zigzag fashion. Around this they tied a string of red horsehair, finally thrusting a number of eagle-tail feathers into a cornhusk ring, fastened to the back of the disk. In fact, they prepared a sun symbol as it is still worn on the back of the flute players in the Flute ceremony. Then they placed this symbol on the white cloth again, again asked some one to stand on it, and, as in the case of the moon, they swung the cloth with its contents into the air, where it kept twirling upward and upward towards the east. Soon they again saw a light rising in the east. It became brighter and brighter and warmer. That proved to be the sun, and it had not come up very high when the Hopi already felt its warmth.

After the sun had been created and was rising day after day, the people were very happy, because it was now warm and very light, so that they could attend to their work very well. The children ran around and played. They now thought of moving on. They had a great many provisions by this time, and so the chiefs again met in a council to talk the matter over. So the people started. The White People took a southern route, the Hopi a more northern, and between them travelled the Pueblo Indians of New Mexico. Often certain parties remained at certain places, sometimes for several years. They built houses and plant crops.

With the passing of time, they became estranged from each other, and began to attack and kill one another. When starting, the chiefs had agreed that as soon as one of the parties should reach the place where the sun rises, many stars would fall from the sky, and when that would happen all the travelling parties should remain and settle down where they would be at that time. The White People having taken a southern route; were more gifted than the other people. When they had become very tired carrying their children and their burdens, one of the women bathed and took the scales that she had rubbed off from her body and made horses of these scales. These horses they used after that for travelling, so that they could proceed much faster. In consequence of this they arrived at the place where the sun rose before any of the other parties arrived there. And immediately many stars fell from the sky. Then they settled down where they were. It had also been agreed upon before the different parties started; that whenever enemies should molest those who had not reached the place where the sun rises, they should notify those who had arrived at the sunrise, and the latter, would then come and help them.

The Hopi Gods and the Kachina Cult

To Hopi people one of the most sacred aspects of their daily life is their religion. This religion is called Kachina. The Hopi religious dogma is precise, the ceremonial round is exacting, and the kachinas play a vital ceremonial role. To maintain the balance in nature and to sustain man's relationship with the gods each individual is obligated to contribute to the best of his ability. An individual's contribution is manifested in being 'hopi' or good. The anticipated behaviour for an indi-vidual is dealt in detail because being 'hopi' involved more than goodness alone. The ideal Hopi is considered to be cooperative, self-effacing, and non aggressive. He has moral as well as physical strength and good health. He accepts collective re-sponsibilities and concentrates on good thoughts. Conversely, an evil or bad person is called 'kahope,' with personality traits opposite to those of the ideal Hopis.

The Hopis consider that Kachinas are the spirit essence of everything in this real world. They also believe that these Kachinas possess a large amount of wisdom and power that can be compared to the wisdom of a religious and learned elder. They are small, painted and adorned wooden images usually made by men prior to kachina performances. The figures are presented to children by kachinas and are considered by them as gifts from the gods. These kachina images are also hung from the rafters of the homes to familiarize the children with the many different forms. Kachina figures frequently are called dolls, but this is a mis-nomer. They are not mere toys but serve mainly to instruct uninitiated children about one aspect of the religious system. There are over 240 different forms that are made by the Hopi; they fit into six groups, including chief kachinas, clowns, and guards. A figure is carved from cottonwood tree roots, shaped, and then smoothed before appendages such as ears or horns are pegged in place. A thin layer of white clay is applied, and the clay is painted in vivid colours, the same ones used for the body paintings of real kachinas. Finally feather adornments are often added to complete the figure.

Six groups of Kachinas

Chief Kachina - A chief Kachina belongs solely to a particular clan. The Chief Kachinas is considered to be the most important class of Kachinas. The Alohi clan is an example of a chief Kachina.

Guard Kachina - The guard Kachina protects the tribe and enforces rules.

Clown Kachina - Clown Kachinas provide amusement during Kachina holy social ceremonies. Many times the actions of the clowns are meant to portray a lesson on improper behaviour apparent in a tribal member.

The Other Three Types of Kachinas:

1. Supernatural Beings - These Kachinas live in or around Flagstaff, Arizona. These supernatural Kachinas are said to unknowingly dispense 'spiritual and physical favours to deserving Hopi.'

2. Human Personification - During Hopi ceremonies the men of the tribe wear costumes and masks that closely resemble the Kachina that is being honoured. To the Hopi, these men serve as intermediaries between the spiritual and natural worlds. In the eyes of the Hopi, the Kachina dancers become the true human personification of the spirits. The ceremonies involving the Kachinas are extremely sacred. The Hopi believe that these ceremonial acts serve many purposes, such as bringing good weather and bountiful harvest. Participation in ritual ceremonies is vital to the Kachina religion, as a prayer or an observance isn't enough. The majority of the ceremonies are held in kivas that are underground ceremonial sites.

3. Dolls or Tihus – The Hopi girls receive two dolls each year, from about one-year old until they are ten. The dolls are only given to the women because the women of the tribe do not possess the same degree of contact with the supernatural as the men of the tribe do. Therefore, the men who dance and impersonate different Kachinas, carve small wooden replicas of them and present them to infants and girls.

Another purpose of these dolls is to familiarize the children with the different Kachina spirits. They also help to keep kids in line, as is represented in the Ogre Woman Kachina. This Kachina goes door to door before the bean dance demanding food. She leaves the Hopi girls a couple grains of corn and says that she will be back, and if she isn't given food she will take the children. When she comes back she asks the children if they have been bad. Sometimes she will begin to pull the children by their feet to give them the idea that she is going to eat them. Before she can take them away a relative appeases the Ogre by telling her that the child has learned her lesson, and that it will never happen again. The moral of the story is that children learn that they must work hard and do all they can to contribute to the food supply. As such the Kachinas serve in social discipline and reform too.

Kachina carvings are styled renditions of the disguises worn by the men. Participation as a kachina is open to all village men under the general sanction of the Village Chief, and the activities of kachinas are under the con-trol of the Badger and Kachina clans. The head of a kachina impersonator is covered with a basketry or leather mask, and he peers through small holes that have no relationship to the eyes on the mask. Noses are highly styled protuberances, and mouths may be tubular, beak-shaped, or painted in various ways onto the flat mask. The top of a mask is often adorned with a wooden tablet, feathers, hair, or wool. A fox-skin encircles the neck where the mask meets the body. A wide variety of costumes such as a white cotton shirt, cotton kilt, sash, and green moccasins are common for chief kachinas. Vivid colourful paints applied to the bodies of the impersonators makes them even more striking. Colours symbolize the direction from which the kachina came. The colour yellow stands for north, blue-green for west, red for south; white for east; while red, yellow, white and blue-green in combination indicate the zenith, and black for the nadir. The mask, body, and legs are often painted with represen-tations of heavenly phenomena, animal tracks, and phallic or vegetable sym-bols. These vivid colours of gods are a striking contrast to the drab desert setting and the bland colours found in the village environment.

Legend of Kachinas

According to Tawaqwaptiwa, the late Village Chief of Oraibi, the legend says that once long ago, after the Hopi had departed from the uppermost level of the un-derworld they wandered on earth with their gods the kachinas. Then the Mexicans attacked them and all the gods were killed. The dead returned to the underworld, and the Hopi divided their ceremonial rituals in order to impersonate them during the year. These impersonations of kachinas form the core of Hopi rituals. When a man wears the sacred costume of a kachina, he becomes a god, and his mask is the most sacred thing of his costume. As masks wear out, become soiled, or break, they are replaced or repaired, but this does not reduce their sacredness. The chief kachina masks are the only ones not replaced or duplicated. It is also possible to vary a new kachina mask from the original without impairing its supernatural associations. Kachinas are present at Oraibi from the winters to the summers, and then they are in the underworld except for Masau'u Kachina, representing the God of Death, who remains on the earth for the whole year. A Hopi adult does not believe that an impersonator is a god but rather considers his role as a friend of the gods. Small children by contrast are told that these were the actual gods.

Intimacy with forces of nature

The complexities of Kachina worship are of a little concern to the Hopi. They make no effort to classify their beliefs, but are content to regard the Kachinas as a host of benevolent spirits who have the best interests of the Hopi always at heart. To impersonate them is a pleasure, to observe them a delight for the Hopi. Quite apart from its more formal features, the opera-tion of the Kachina cycle brings more warmth and colour into the lives of the Hopi than any other aspect of their culture.

The relationship of people, with the gods, forms an orderly system built around the concept of continuity between life and death. An integrated relationship is maintained between the living and the dead, with the spirits of the dead becoming clouds that bring rain to the living. The activities of kachinas on earth and in the underworld benefit the living Hopi. To the Hopi there is a duality in being human. People possess a physical body and a 'breath-body,' quite resembling to the concept of spirit or soul. When an individual dies, preparations for burial are in many ways the same as for the newborn. Since the corpse is sprinkled with cornmeal, bathed, and given a new name. The breath-body journeys to the underworld, where its existence is like that of the Hopi on earth, except that when the dead consume food they take only the essence of it. Because of their weightlessness the dead could rise into the sky and become clouds. By bringing rain, the deceased aid the living in a very meaningful manner. The God of Death, Masau'u, logically is a god of fertility since rain lead to fertility and growth. The sun, also a god of fertil-ity, has an intimate association with the dead. The sun spends half of its time in the underworld, the land of the dead, and half of its time on earth. It is by prayers and offerings to the dead and to the sun that blessings are real-ised on earth.

Dual concepts integrate Hopi society still further. An individual that is born to this earth, after death he is born to the underworld, only again to 'die' in the underworld and become reborn on earth. Even in death, the breath--bodies are capable of returning to earth. As there is an earthly life cycle for an individual, there is a daily and yearly cycle for the sun too. Each morning the sun leaves its eastern home and at sunset enters its western home; thus it furnishes light equally to the earth and the underworld. On a yearly basis, winter begins with the summer solstice and ends with the winter solstice, while summer begins about mid-December and lasts until about mid-June. The winter solstice on earth is a summer solstice in the underworld, and the reverse also is true. The Hopi believe that when a major ceremony is being held on earth, a minor one is celebrated in the underworld by the kachinas. As it is ex-pected, death in theory holds no fears, for the living and the dead are considered one.

Other Deities

The Hopi know one all-wise and good spirit, named Cotukinuniwa, 'The Heart of the Stars.' They also have Balikokon, the Great Water Snake, the spirit of the element of water, and they see him in the rains and snows, the rivers and springs, the sap in the trees and the blood in the body. The whole Hopi heavens are filled, too, with Kachina, angels. All the great dead men of the Hopi nation saw Kachina and received messages from them, some time before they died. And some of the chiefs now living have seen them, too. As it is so often found in the religion of a people who are low in mental development, and in whose pitiful lives the hours of trial and privation and sorrow are much more numerous than the happy ones, the spirit of good, though all-wise, is not all-powerful, so it is found here. Cotukinuniwa loves his children and would send to them nothing but good, but that he cannot always do, for Balilokon is sometimes stronger than him, and is evil. Yet it would not be right to call Balilokon the spirit of evil, for he is not always so. When he is pleases, the mists and rains fall gently and the sap runs lustily through plants and trees, giving them vigorous growth; the springs and rivers are full giving abundance of good water to the people and their flocks, and the blood flowing in the veins of the children of the tribe is the blood of health; but Balilokon is sometimes angered and the rains does not come at all, or comes in deluges that destroy; the rivers are dry or are raging floods; the sap is withdrawn from the plants and trees and they die, and the blood of the people flows through their veins but to poison. There have been times when the anger of Balilokon it seemed no ceremony or prayer could appease; then hundreds of the people were drowned to death, and one time, away in the dim past he sent a great flood that covered nearly all the earth, and very few of the people and not many of the beasts were saved. Balilokon, having it in his power to do so much of evil, is the god most prayed to, and in his name almost all the ceremonies are held. At the foot of the cliff at the southern point of the mesa is a large rock with a nearly flat top, about eight feet in size, and a few yards to one side of it is a well worn trail. This is called the Hopi luck shrine. On the top of the rock are thousands of pebbles, and around the base are other thousands that have fallen. It is the great luck stone, and since long time the children of the villages go there to get forecasts of their lives. Each little devotee of the blind goddess selects three pebbles, and while walking down the trail, throws them, one by one, upon the rock. If but one pebble lodges, the thrower will know much of sorrow and disappointment, yet his efforts will sometimes bear good fruits. If two pebbles stay he will find more than the average of success, and if all three lodge upon the top he may march onward boldly. The Hopi worship or devotional acts are largely private. Their communal and public worship are generally by dancing or in games.

Symbolizations of gods

The number and variety of idols or images belonging to the Hopi community is startling. In every household there can be seen, one to a dozen wooden or clay idols or gods of the oddest and quaintest shapes, roughly made, and while resembling one another, they are different from any other Indian images. They are of all sizes, from two inches to over four feet high, painted in various colours; sometimes they are dressed with beautiful ceremonial robes, woven expressly for them. These gods are not gods at all, but represent different kachinas who are but semi-gods and intermediaries between the Hopis and their principal deity.

The kachinas figures are found suspended to the beams that support the roofs of Hopi dwellings or tucked away in little niches or standing up in rows on stone shelves. They are male and female, some vigorously pronounced; the females have extraordinary headdresses only, but the males are most modestly decorated. The male is called O-mow and the female A-to-se-ka. These gods are used during the ceremonies. All possess great antiquity, and when not in use are hidden away by their custodians where they cannot be found by anyone who is not in charge of them.

The gods are also made from trunks or limbs of small trees, which by chance have grown to resemble in part of a human body. Such figures are regarded with great favour. It is believed that the spirit of a kachina was in such a wood. The material employed in making the kachina are the clothes being of white cotton cloth, richly embroidered in colours; the headdress made of feathers. The colours employed in making these gods are not used with any regard to rule, but as each individual fancies.

These kachina 'dolls' have attracted widespread atten-tion from whites and have been collected avidly for many years. Over the years other Indians and many non-Indians have begun carving and selling Kachina carvings and dolls.

Sorcery

The origin of witchcraft is traced to Spider Woman, who caused the first human death. Hopi believe that each typical village includes more witches than ordinary people. Witches may be male or female and from any clan; no one is considered to be incapable of witch-craft. A Village Chief or ceremonial leader may be a suspect simply because he holds an important office. Any self-assertive person is open to the accusa-tion of being a witch because such behavior is not Hopi. It is possible to become a witch either by voluntarily practicing sorcery or by unknowingly being inducted into a society of witches as a child. In the latter instance, exist-ing witches reportedly carry off a related child while it sleeps and induct it into a secret society that follows the patterning of other Hopi secret societies. The initiate is then said to have taught the witches' art of assuming the shape of an animal to pursue their evil craft by night. The power of a witch is derived from association with a familiar animal, such as a coyote, owl, wolf, or small black ant, from whom the greatest forces of evil emanate; quite logically, sorcerers possess 'two hearts,' their own and that of their familiar animal. Sorcerers work evil by causing land erosion, or by driving off rain clouds and replacing them with a windstorm. A Witch is not content with destroying crops but kills people as well. Murder probably is the most important activity of a sorcerer because the Hopis believe that by this, he extends his own life by killing one relative each year. A relative is killed or his illness caused by shooting stiff deer hairs, ants, a bit of bone, or some other object into his body without breaking the skin.

Ordinary people protect themselves against a witch, by wearing arrow points of stone. These are regarded as the ends of lightning flashes associated with the clouds. The Hopi do not attempt to interfere with the activities of witches because they believe that they would die prematurely or encounter misfortune if they did so. A witch's spirit thirsts and hungers for the underworld and approaches it by one step a year. It is said that the sanctions against a witch are not in this world but in the underworld; when his- or her spirit arrives there, it is burned in an oven and becomes a beetle.

Religious Ceremonies

Every religious system requires a series of annual and bi-annual ceremonies to be held by particular religious associations or societies. Among the Hopi community, there are three main ceremonies during the year that involve Kachinas. From December to July the Hopi villages come to life with different Kachina ceremonies. The first major ceremony is Soyal. During this ceremony Kachinas emerge from the kivas slowly as though they have been sleeping for a very long time. The dancers perform rites that are meant to strengthen the Hopi tribe for the upcoming harvest. The second major ceremony occurs in late February. This ceremony is referred to as the Powamu, or the Bean Dance. The significance of this ceremony is the filling of hearts with a hope for a successful germination of the crops to be planted later in the spring. During this ceremony dancers distribute bean sprouts that have been grown in heated kivas prior to the ceremony.

The third ceremony occurs in late July when the first maize of the season is ripe. This celebration is called the Home Dance.

Following this ceremony the Kachinas return to their winter home in the mountains. This ceremony is a way for the Hopi to give thanks to the many Kachinas who have assisted them with their crops. During this ceremony, corn, melons, and fruit are carried by the dancers; as a proof of a bountiful harvest.

Each important ceremony is controlled by a particular organization that is linked to a different clan. A male elder of the leading lineage in each clan usually heads the religious association of his clan. In the possession of the clan a bundle named as the 'mother' or 'heart' of the clan, which consists of an ear of maize, feathers, and coverings, as well as other sacred objects is carried. There is an associate kiva where services are usually held. Rituals are conducted at times established by phases of the moon, the location of the sun when it rose, or the number of days since another ritual ended. The patterning for all the major ceremonies is similar. The rituals span over a period of nine days, and when kiva members are so oc-cupied, a flag is attached to the kiva ladder to warn off the kahopi 'the evil ones.' During the rituals there is a prohibition against eating rich fatty food, meat, and salt. Sexual activities are also restricted before as well as during the time of these celebrations. The first day is a perfunctory beginning; the next eight days are divided into two four-day segments, with the final day usually devoted to a public ritual. The Hopi ceremonies include the use of altars and associated wooden, stone, or clay tablets. On the tablets there are painted motifs symbolic of animals, clouds, maize, and rain. Prayer offerings are left at the proper shrines. Sand paintings and certain fluids with a water base are also considered important. Each secret society is associated with curing of a particular disease. Initiation rituals usually take place around the midpoint of the ceremony and involve washing one's head with yucca suds as well as being given a new name by a ritual sponsor who is already a member of the society.

Ceremonial Secret Societies

To benefit by all the advantages of being a Hopi in this and the un-derworld it is essential for every one to participate actively in the affairs of one or more secret societies. At about nine years of age boys and girls are initiated into either the Kachina Society or the Powamu Society. The Powamu Society is a bit more re-stricted in membership. Within the next few years a girl is expected to join the Lakon, Marau, or Oaqol society; boys join the Antelope, Blue Flute, Gray Flute, or Snake society. It is occasionally that a woman joins a man's society and vice versa to fulfil a particular role. But on the whole, the ceremonial socie-ties are divided along sexual lines. When a boy reaches adolescence, he is expected to undergo the Tribal Initiation; only then he is free to participate in the most sacred of all ceremonies, which is named the Soyal.

The annual ritual calendar is considered to begin with winter solstice or Soyal Ceremony. The Soyal is conceived around that mysterious moment of the year when, in Hopi thinking, the sun rises at the same place for four days, and the days are shortest. Only the men, who have completed the Tribal Initiation, conduct the Soyal Ceremony. At Oraibi the Wuwutcim Society conducts the most sacred of the Soyal rituals, and it is far more popular than the others. This society is composed of Bear clan members and is directed by the village chief. The principal purpose of the ceremony is to compel the sun to begin the trip back to its summer home so that it would bring warmth that would help for the crops to be planted. The climax of the rituals comes when the 'Star Priest,' called Sun Priest at other times, per-forms a dance representing the cycle of the sun. The ceremony has the com-plementary purposes of inducing fertility in both women and plants, and par-ticipation is village-wide. The kachinas and particular men and women dancers perform the sacred dance. The typical smoking and prayers are accompanied by the offering of a large number of diverse prayer offerings of cornhusks, feathers, and prayer sticks.

The other Powamu Ceremony begins when the February new moon is seen first. It climaxes in the forced growth of beans in the kiva of the Powamu Society. Each man raises fifty to one hundred bean plants in his own kiva. The beans are well watered, and the kiva fires burned hot day and night to force the sprouting. The sprouted beans are cut and bundled to be presented by kachinas to the grower's uninitiated offspring, his ceremonial children, and favoured relatives. If a child is to be initiated into the Powamu Society, he sees the sacred rituals for the first time on the fifth day. This new knowledge is not to be revealed, under threat of punishment by the kachinas. By undergoing the initiation, participants become members of the Powamu Society and are permitted to impersonate kachinas, to partici-pate in kachina rituals, and to become kachina fathers or ceremonial sponsors. Not all children are inducted into the Powamu Society; the remaining children are inducted into the Kachina Society on the sixth day of the Powamu ceremony.

In August, there is another high point on the ceremonial ground is reached with the performances of the Antelope-Snake or Blue and Gray Flute society ceremonies on alternate years. The Antelope and Snake societies are separate or-ganizations, but they combine for their major annual ceremony. The two societies offer prayer offerings jointly. Then they go to their respective kivas, where they perform secret rituals. At this time the Snake Society members collect snakes from each of the four directions on four different days. At a proper time a Snake man receives a snake that he holds by his lips or teeth just behind the snake's head. He dances around the plaza several times while a partner brushes his shoulders with a 'snake whip,' which is a short stick with eagle feathers attached on it. Each snake is danced with and then released on the ground at the plaza. The snakes then are gathered together in a circle and sprinkled with corn meal by females of the Snake clan. Finally, younger men of the Snake So-ciety pick up as many snakes as they could handle and take them to shrines in each of the four cardinal directions.

These public performances of Snake Society members have attracted more popular interest among the people around the world than any other American Indian ritual. The reason is that the snake dancers carried prairie rattlesnakes in their mouths as often as they carry harmless species such as the bull snake. Snake Society members handle poisonous and harmless snakes with equal ease. Illness or death from snakebite among the dancers is unreported, and various explanations have been offered concerning the Indians ability to handle poisonous snakes. The Hopi even do not have an effective antidote for venom, which is proven by laboratory tests of their snake medi-cine.

The final ceremony of major importance is the Tribal Initiation. This is con-trolled and conducted by the Agaves Society. It is held only when this society has at least one candidate for initiation. During this ceremony adolescent males are ini-tiated into one of four secret societies, the Agaves, Horns, Singers, or Wuwut-cim. A male cannot be a fully participating adult in Hopi society until he has passed through this initiation. The Tribal Initiation is the most complex of the ceremonies and a cornerstone of Hopi religion. It takes place in November at a time established by the sun's position. A new fire is first burned in the Agave kiva, by the kiva chief, and some embers are carried to the other participating kivas. Then an idol called Dawn Woman is brought from her shrine and exhibited on top of the kivas until the fifth day of the cer-emony. Then she is returned to her shrine after 'delivering' her offspring. All candidates sleep in their kivas, and the dances that are performed on the third and fifth days are clearly associated with fertility, with phallic symbols and simulated pregnancies presented. These events, and many others, symbolize the ritual rebirth of male children into manhood and reaffirm the integration between the living and the dead.

Participation in secret societies is not restricted to men. The Hopi women also control three voluntary religious associations, the Lakon, Marau, and Oaqol. Just as the secret societies of men include a few women, so the religious associations of the women include a few males. The organization of women's societies is similar to that of males. They are controlled by a lineage in a particular clan, possessing bundles, carrying out secret rituals in a kiva, and per-forming certain ceremonies in public.

Marriage and related rituals

The Hopi form of courtship and marriage is also very simple. There are neither priests nor civil officials to do anything with it. When a young man seeks a wife he pays court to a maiden of his own choosing, and if he is favoured she sends him a basket of variously coloured peki, which signifies that she is willing to marry him. Then he, with all his people, visits her family, and they altogether have a little feast. After the relatives of a couple approve a match, the girl grounds maize for three days at the groom's house to demonstrate her abilities as a home-maker. There is no comparable trial for the groom. While the girl is in the boy's home, his paternal aunts attack the boy's mother and her sisters with mud and water for permitting the girl to 'steal' their sweet boy. The fight is held in an atmosphere of jovial hostility. On the morning of the fourth day, their respective mothers and female rela-tives wash the couples' hair in one container. A mingling of their hair symbolizes their marital union. Once again the paternal aunts of the boy attempt halfheartedly to disrupt the ritual. After their hair dry, the couple stands at the cliff edge to pray to the sun and later returns to the groom's home for a wedding breakfast. They are now man and wife, but they continue to live in the groom's house until his male relatives and any other men who offer to help complete the bride's wedding costume. The men prepare the cotton and weave two sets of wedding garments, a small robe, and a white-fringed belt; in addition they prepare skins and sew white moccasins and leggings. During the manufacture of these items the groom's family feasts the workers. After about a month, the garments are completed; the bride returns home wearing one set and carrying the second in a reed container. Her husband takes up residence in her household. The wedding garments are very important because they are said to be required for entering the underworld after death. Any form of plural marriage is prohibited. These people are very moral and hold in most sacred regard the family life. They do not marry sisters or cousins, and they invariably go out of their family to select wives or husbands. Among the Hopi, it is believed that there is a great spirit, who lives in the sun and who gives them light and heat. With the Hopi there are male and female in the idea of deity; the earth is the female, and all living things are the issue.

Death rituals

The Hopi people bury their dead with much ceremony. They do not put them in boxes or coffins, but wrap them in blankets and lay them away in the rocks with bowls of sacred meal, meat, water, corn, and fruits. This is not done from any superstitious notion that these things are going to be of any use to the dead, but because they are symbols of certain ideas. The women are the chief mourners and are grief stricken at their loss. The great altitude of the town with the consequently rare and pure air prevents odours. Men who attend the dead purify themselves afterwards by washing in a boiled preparation, and there is a ritual in the household of the deceased to protect members against spirits. The next day the man who has offered the prayer takes cornmeal and five prayer-sticks to the grave. The prayer sticks are believed to help the person on his travels to the land of the dead, and the food is to feed the spirit. A prayer is offered, and the spirit is told not to return for anyone else in the community. All possessions of the deceased are thrown away. A sepa-rate cemetery is provided for the stillborn, infants, and children. The Hopis believe that the spirit of an infant does not travel to the underworld but lingers above the house, to be reborn again as a person of the opposite sex. While the death of an adult is sur-rounded with misgivings and fear in spite of the fact that most dead are to be reborn into a peaceful world which is an intimate part of the Hopi religion.

An overall study of the Hopi religious system reveals that it is a finely tuned totality. The kachinas always fulfil their obligations in the un-der world, and if the Hopi on earth does the same, there is no hardship or unhappiness. It is the responsibility of each person to fulfil his or her social ceremonial obligations as being a Hopi. Community-wide prosperity indi-cates that each individual has contributed his or her utmost, and the ideals of the Hopi are thus achieved. The Hopi ritual is extraordinarily complex and time-consuming, and the paraphernalia required is extensive. Although ‘he Hopi cult has become highly modified by a semi-arid environment, it consists originally of ancestor worship, embracing worship of the great powers of nature — sky, sun, moon, fire, rain, and earth. A confusion of effect and cause and an elaboration of the doctrines of signatures pervade all their rites, which in the main may be regarded as sympathetic magic.

****

CHAPTER-4

ZOROASTRIANISM

The development of the religion of the tribes of Persia had been in a very special manner. It emerged in a form that was much different from the religion of other ancient eastern tribes.

This religion is known to the world by several names: Mazda religion (In the name of Ahura Mazda, the principal god of the pantheon), Zoroastrianism (In the name of the founder prophet, Zoroaster), Avesta religion (In the name of the major scripture, the Zend Avesta) and also as the Fire Worship religion (because of their fire rituals).

Because of the lack of ancient scriptures, the study of the development of this Persian religion is quite difficult. The reference that we find in the accounts of ancient Greek classical writer, Herodotus is insufficient. So we have to depend wholly on the available books of this religion itself to know the story of its development.

Development

It is believed that in the second millennium B.C., people in Persia were divided into the ancient Persians and Indian Aryans. Before this happened, both the communities resembled each other in language and culture. Their religious rituals were also similar. This view is cleared by the study of the Vedas too. In the Zend Avesta, we find the worship of the dead ancestors that is the same as in the Vedas. The Persians considered cow as a holy animal, this thought also resembles that of the Aryans. Both of them worshipped fire and the heavenly elixir.

On this basis, Zoroastrianism developed among the ancient Persians. Legend says that prophet Zoroaster wrote Zend Avesta in the sixth century B.C. The date of Zoroaster's birth is uncertain. Legend says that he was pre-existent and born of a fifteen-year-old virgin in 660 B.C. Many marvels accompanied his birth. His name, Zarathustra Spitama, indicates he was born into a warrior clan that was connected with the royal family of ancient Persia. At fifteen he put on the kusti, a sacred string belt symbolic of his passage into manhood as a member of his religion. He spent years, partially in solitude, searching for answers to his religious quests. At the age of thirty Zoroaster had a vision of the angel Vohu Mana, who appeared nine times the size of a man. The angel told him that there was only one true God, Ahura Mazda, and that he was to become the prophet of Ahura Mazda. During the next ten years Zoroaster had other visions in which each of the archangels of Ahura Mazda appeared and revealed further truth to him.

He began preaching this new revelation but with no success. In ten years the only convert he won was his cousin. But the turning point came when he met the Aryan King Vishtaspa. In a struggle with local priests he was thrown in jail but after two years won Vishtaspa to his faith by his wondrous cure of Vishtaspa's favourite black horse. The king put all of his power behind the propagation of the faith. Thus Zoroaster became a leader in the nation and married three wives and was the father of six children.

The next twenty years were spent vigorously promulgating the faith among Persians and fighting two holy wars in its defence. During a war with the Turanians an enemy soldier found the seventy-seven year old prophet Zoroaster tending the sacred flame in a fire temple and killed him.

Curiosities about the religion of ancient Persia were formed long ago, and it was the old foe of Persia, the Greek, who first studied it. Aristotle, Hermippus; and many others wrote about it in their books. But, only a few fragments of such scriptures are available to the modern world. The more detailed and important information about it is found scattered in the accounts of ancient historians and travellers, which have extended over a period of ten centuries, from Herodotus down to Agathias and Procopius. Then during the first centuries of the Christian era, it was studied with much more interest and enthusiasm. But at that time, the religion of Persia was more studied and less understood than it had ever been before. The real object was aimed at, in studying the old religion to make a ground for a new one.

Throughout the middle ages nothing was known of Zoroastrianism, except the name of its founder, who from a Magus was converted into a magician and was a master of the hidden sciences. It was then that during the Renaissance the real inquiry was resumed. The first step regarding that was to collect all the information that could be gathered from the classics of the ancient Greek and Roman writers. Later, many Italian, English, and French travellers went in search of truth and at last found Zoroaster's last followers in Persia and India. They were the one who revealed their existence, their manners, and the main features of their belief to the rest of the world.

It is noticed that the religion bears a great deal of resemblance with the Hindu religion of India. It is also found that Zoroastrianism is a medley of Vedic and Islamic tales. So, on one hand, Zoroastrianism is the one out of which Mohammed formed his religion, and on the other hand the old religions of India and Persia flow from a common source.

This religion flourished over Persia at the time, when the second successor of Mohammed overthrew the Sassanian dynasty. In less than a century after their defeat, nearly all the conquered people were brought over to the faith of their new rulers, either by force, or policy, or the attractive power of a simpler form of creed. But many of those who clung to the faith of their fathers, went and sought a new home abroad, where they might freely worship their old gods, say their holy prayers, and perform their old sacred rites. At last, they found their home among the tolerant Hindus, on the western coast of India. There they still live, while the social and religious ranks of their fellow religionists in Persia are daily dwindling away.

Legend of Creation

The Zend Avesta, the sacred writings of the Parsees, states that the Supreme Being Ahura Mazda (Ormuzd), created the universe and man in six successive periods of time.

The Avesta account of the Creation is limited to this announcement, but we find a more detailed history of the origin of human species a book named 'Bundaehisn,' which is dedicated to the exposition of a complete cosmogony. This book states that the duration of the life on earth is conceived of as a sort of cosmic year, consisting of 12,000 calendar years divided into four periods of 3000 years each.

Zoroastrianism was a dualistic religion according to which two spirits were thought to exist right from the eternity. One was Ohrmazd (Ahura Mazda) the supreme god and the other was Ahreman (Angra Mainiiu). Ohrmazd was a good power, residing on high in the infinite light. While Ahreman, endowed with 'knowledge after the fact' and a desire for destruction, resided in the abyss in infinite darkness. There was an atmosphere between both of them, where the mixture of the two spirits took place. In his omniscience Ohrmazd knew that Ahreman existed and that he would attack sooner or later. Ohrmazd made the creation to serve as his instrument in the battle. He made it in spiritual form from his own essence, the material light. The creation consisted of everything from gods to primal man. It was kept in spiritual form for 3000 years, during which the creatures remained in the spiritual state, 'unthinking and stable.' At the same time Ahreman made his demonic creatures out of darkness.

Then Ahreman rose up to the border between the two worlds, saw the light, and desired it. Ohrmazd offered peace to Ahreman but Ahreman rejected the offer and threatened to take over the entire universe. Then Ohrmazd recited the Ahunwar thus: Yatha ahu vairyo ('as a heavenly lord is to be chosen') and uttered the twenty-one sacred words. When one of its three parts was uttered, the evil spirit contracted his body through fear, and when two parts of it were uttered he fell upon his knees, and when all of it was uttered he became confounded and impotent. Thus Ohrmazd revealed to Ahreman his own final victory and the impotence of Ahreman. This followed the destruction of the demons, the resurrection of the dead and the freedom from opposition to the creatures forever and ever. When Ahreman saw his own impotence together with the destruction of the demons he lost consciousness and fell back into the darkness and laid there unconscious for the next 3000 years.

After this initial victory over Ahreman, during a 3000-year recess, Ohrmazd then made his creation in material form. The first of Ohrmazd's creatures of the world was the sky, and his good thought (Vohuman), by good procedure, produced the light of the world, along with which was the good religion of the Mazdayasnians; this was because the renovation (Frashegird) which happens to the creatures was known to him! Afterwards arose Ardwahisht, and then Shahrewar, and then Spandarmad, and then Hordad, and then Amurdad. From the light and freshness of the sky he made the seed of men and bulls and put it in the bodies of the primal bull and primal man so that they would have abundant progeny. After 3000 years Ahreman was finally aroused from his unconsciousness by the primal whore's recounting to him what she intended to do to Ohrmazd's creation. Ahreman was comforted and attacked the creation, starting by dragging the sky down from the station of the stars into the intermediate atmosphere. He afflicted pollution on the waters and the fire and assaulted humanity with suffering, misery, disease, and death. Thirty years after the attack, the first man was killed, his seed fell into the earth, and from this a plant germinated from which the two first humans, Masi and Masyani were born.

Meities and Demons

The Deities worshipped by the ancient Aryans are the common property of both the branches, the Hindu Aryans and the Persian Aryans. These may be divided into two classes: the first containing those names which came to signify diametrically opposed powers among the two communities, and the second which contains names of Deities who are regarded as benefices by both. The older scholars seemed to think that Zoroaster came as a reformer, and that out of a host of Gods he put forward only Ahura as the One Supreme God. This caused a religious conflict which led to the inversion of some of the ancient Deities into Demons among the Iranians, and that the Hindus also repaid the compliment. Apparently there was a religious conflict, but the origin of it could by no means be ascribed to Zoroaster with any degree of certainty.

Zoroaster taught that Ahura Mazda (also known by many other names) was the one true God and the nature gods or daevas (devils) his people worshipped were false gods. Ahura Mazda reveals himself to man through six modes (called archangels by Western). Three were masculine and three were feminine in nature. Together with Ahura Mazda they compose seven sources of reality. The masculine immortals are Asha (knowledge of the law of God), Vohu-Mana (love), and Kshathra (loving service). The three feminine immortals are Armaiti (piety), Haurvatat (wholeness or perfection) and Ameretat (immortality).

The Avesta religion is based on the concept of 'Dualism'. It believes that both bright and dark elements are present in the nature. The dark elements cause the origin of the evil forces while the bright one is the cause of the origin of good forces. Among the bright ones, Ahura Mazda is considered the greatest. Under him are six above-mentioned immortal powers. Then come the several other good powers along with the angels.

Ahura Mazda: The very first name that occurs in this connection is that of the Supreme Lord Himself-Ahura-which in the Sanskrit from Asura signifies 'a demon'. The name originally signifies 'the Lord of Life' (from Av. ahu, Skt. asu, life), or the One Life from which all proceed. The Sanskrit Asura also signifies originally the One Eternal Life, and in the Rig-Veda (in its oldest portions) it is not used in its later degraded signification. In classical Sanskrit the name Purva-devah (earlier Gods) is also used for the Asuras; and the legend has grown up in India that it was these Asuras who had once ruled the Earth, till in later ages they were ousted from their positions by the comparatively more modern Devas (gods). In the earlier Vedas the epithet Asura is used especially for Varuna, the Ruler of the endless Heavenly Sphere, refulgent by day and shining with innumerable stars at night. Varuna is also the All-pervading Life that powers the Creation. He is the Ruler of the universe; the Lord of righteousness, the One Being who has laid down the Law and Order of Nature, and is the Father of All. The one important point to be noted is that in Vedic context there is a great emphasis, laid on the moral and ethical aspect of this God. Varuna is pre-eminently the Lord of Righteousness. This grand concept of Asura Varuna agrees closely with that of Ahura-Mazda of the earlier Avesta; and very probably the legends in the Vedas and in the Epics of the Hindus about conflicts between 'the Gods and the Demons' are but echoes of some religious and national strife between the two branches of the Aryans in the prehistoric days. Ahura Mazda ("Lord Wisdom") was the supreme god, he who created the heavens and the Earth, and another son of Zrvan Akarana. As leader of the Heavenly

Host, the Amesha Spentas, he battles Ahriman and his followers to rid the world of evil, darkness and deceit. He is symbolised by a winged disc.

The Avestic Daeva is the natural complement of Ahura. Originally 'the Shining One', this word retains its purity practically throughout the history of Indian languages. But in the Avesta the word is never used in its old signification of 'Deity', even in the earliest portions, and in the later Avesta it invariably means 'Demon'. In the Vedas however, this word is used for a few times as an epithet of the demons.

There are a few individual deities who have suffered this inversion. The most notable of them is Indra, one of the greatest Deities in the Vedic Pantheon. In the Avesta he is the chief helpmate of the Evil One. It is very remarkable that of two of the most important Gods of the Vedas, Varuna and Indra, one should have become in Iran the Supreme Being, Ahura, while the other became the most important lieutenant of the Evil One.

But what is still more remarkable is that one of Indra's epithets-Vrtrahan (Bahram, the Slayer of the Demon-foe) has continued all through the history of Iranian Religion to be the name of one of the greatest of the Deities, Verethraghna (later Bahram). The Bahram Yasht, where his deeds are recorded, is a fine epic; and some of the achievements therein recorded resemble the account of the deeds of Indra mentioned in the Vedas.

Vayu (the Wind, a name which is identically the same in both the languages): This is another of the ancient Aryan deities. He is the only Vedic Deity who is mentioned by same name in Zoroastrianism.

Nairyosangha: This is the Messenger of the Supreme Ahura Mazda to mankind. He appears before the Great Saviours when the time has arrived for their manifestation in the world. One of his special tasks is 'the guarding of the seed of Zarathushtra' from which the future Redeemers of mankind are to be born. He is also said to have helped at the creation of the first human couple, the Masi and Masyani. In the Avesta he represents some kind of Divine Fire, and in the Veda's, under the name Narashamsa (he who is praised of mankind) he also represents the Sacred Fire.

Armaiti: This is the Spirit of the Earth, and also of Divine Wisdom and Grace, both in the Avesta and in the Vedas. She has the rank of an Amesha-Spenta (a Holy Immortal, corresponding to an Archangel in Christianity) in the Zoroastrianism. In the Avesta she also represents the Spirit of Obedience to the Eternal Law of God and also in a few passages in the Rig-Veda she represents the same idea. But on the whole her position in the Veda is much humbler than in the Avesta, for in the latter she is represented as the Guardian of the Faith of Zarathushtra.

Baga (corresponding to the Vedic Bhaga): This is an epithet of the Supreme Being Ahura Mazda in the Achaemenian inscriptions at Persepolis and elsewhere. In the Veda he is a special Deity who is later identified with the Sun.

Airyaman: This is also one of the ancient Aryan Deities, and in the Veda his name is mainly associated with those of the great Twin-Brethren Mithra and Varuna. To both the nations the name implies for 'friend' or 'comrade' and so he is specially the God presiding over marriage. A similar position is accorded to him in the Veda where he is invoked during the marriage ceremony, and among the Parsis today a short hymn dedicated to him, and called the Airyema-ishyo, is still used as an essential part of the wedding ceremony. He was the Zoroastrian god of friendship and healing.

Mithra: But the most important of the ancient Indo-Iranian Deities in many ways is Mithra, who represents the Sun. He is considered to be a god of light, contracts and friendship. He also maintains the cosmic order. Sometimes mentioned as the son of Ahura Mazda, he assists him in his struggle against the forces of evil, represented by Angra Mainyu. In the Vedas, he is very intimately associated with Asura Varuna. In the Avesta, however, he is associated more with the two Guardian-Judges of departed souls than with Ahura Mazda. He awaits the Souls on the other side of death and sits in Judgment over them by the side of Sraosha and Rashnu. He dwells on the top of the Hara-Bareza (Alborz) Mountain. In the Avesta, he is the Great Being who is the Wise Ruler, the Loving Guardian and the Impartial Judge of humanity, a conception that is essentially ethical. In the Veda too his position is similar. In later days the cult of Mithra attained great importance in the esoteric school of occultism, which in its turn profoundly influenced the later Roman thought as well as earlier Christianity.

Haoma: This is another Indo-Iranian Deity, being the Vedic Soma. In the Avesta he is not a mere personification of the legendary Soma-plant, but a great Teacher who appeared in the very early days to lead forward our infant humanity; and he is represented in the Avesta as being adored by the great Teachers of ancient Iran themselves. In Yasna, he is represented as appearing before Zarathushtra and telling him in broad outline the history of the Sacred Teaching in Iran in the ages gone by. Some scholars believe that it was he who introduced the Haoma- (soma-) Cult among the Aryans and thus gave his own name to the plant and its juice which formed an important item of the Indo-Iranian ritual. The Hindu and Zoroastrian rituals turn entirely upon the offering of the juice of this plant; and two priests called the Zaota (Hota) and the Rathwi (corresponding to the Hindu Adhvaryu) officiated at that ceremony. It is a deified plant in Zoroastrian mythology whose sap, which has anaesthetic qualities, was drunk during sacrifices. This deity ruled over all medicinal herbs and granted immortality. It is associated with the purification of fire, and was believed to have the power of providing husbands for unmarried women.

Among others important deities and demons are:

Aesma Daeva: One of the Daevas, Aesma Daeva ('madness') is the demon of lust and anger, wrath and revenge. He is the personification of violence, a lover of conflict and war. Together with the demon of death, Asto Vidatu, he chases the souls of the deceased when they rise to heaven. His eternal opponent is Sraosa.

Agas: A Zoroastrian demon of illness, one of the Drugs. She personifies evil that is perceived or performed by the eye (her name means 'evil eye').

Ahurani: Ahurani is a water goddess from ancient Zoroastrian mythology. She watches over rainfall as well as standing water. She was invoked for health, healing, prosperity, and growth. She is either the wife or the daughter of the great god of creation and goodness, Ahura Mazda. Her name means "She who belongs to Ahura".

Aka Manah: Aka Manah is one of the Daevas. He is the personification of sensual desire who was sent by Ahriman to seduce the prophet Zarathustra. His eternal opponent is Vohu Manah.

Allatum: The goddess of the underworld in early Zoroastrian mythology.

Anahita: The ancient Zoroastrian water goddess, fertility goddess, and patroness of women, as well as a goddess of war. Her name means "the immaculate one". She is portrayed as a virgin, dressed in a golden cloak, and wearing a diamond tiara (sometimes also carrying a water pitcher). The dove and the peacock are her sacred animals. Anahita is sometimes regarded as the consort of Mithra.

Angra Mainyu: God of darkness, the eternal destroyer of good, personification and creator of evil, bringer of death and disease. He is also known as Ahriman, and his name means "fiendish spirit". He is seen as the personification of evil, he leading the dark forces against the hosts of Spenta Mainyu, the Holy Spirit, who assisted Ahura Mazda, the wise lord, and final victor of the cosmic conflict. Ahriman introduced the frost in winter, heat in summer, all manner of diseases and other ills.

Apam-natat: 'God found in the water' who gives water to the people. He is a son of the water-god Vouru-kasa. Apam-natat has also some military aspects and he keeps in check rebellion.

Apaosa: A demon that brings drought and aridity. He rides on a black, bald horse. Eventually the god Tistrya defeated him.

Arishtat: God of Honesty.

Asman: God of the Sky.

Asto Vidatu: The Zoroastrian demon of death that no human escaped. Together with Aesma Daeva he chases and tries to catch the souls of the deceased with a noose when they rise to heaven.

Atar: The Zoroastrian god of all fire and of purity, son of Ahura Mazda.

Bahram: The Zoroastrian god of the planets and victory. He is the assistant of Sraosa, and helps him when Sraosa raises the soul of the deceased from the body.

Burijas: A war god of the Zoroastrian Kassites.

Bushyasta: In Zoroastrian mythology, the yellow demon of lethargy and sloth. He is the evil genius that causes men to oversleep and to neglect their religious duties.

Buyasta: An ancient Zoroastrian demon of laziness that tries to prevent people from working. He is one of the Daevas.

Daena: The goddess who personifies religion in Zoroastrian mythology. Her name means, 'that which was revealed.' Daena is considered to be the daughter of Ahura Mazda.

Daevas: In ancient Zoroastrian mythology they are demons who cause plagues and diseases and who fight every form of religion. They are the male servants (or followers) of Angra Mainyu, also known as Ahriman. The female servants are called the Drugs.

Together they fight Ahura Mazda (Ormazd) and his Amesha Spentas.

Dhaka: An ancient Zoroastrian god of death and demon of deceit and mendacity. He loves destroying life. Dhaka is usually depicted with three heads, while scorpions and lizards crawl all over his body.

Dena: A Zoroastrian goddess. She is the daughter of Ahura Mazda.

Dev: In Zoroastrian mythology, a demon of enormous power, a ruthless and immoral god of war.

Drug: An ancient Zoroastrian female demon, the representation of the lie. She causes much evil. She is the eternal opponent of Asha vahishta.

Drvaspa: The ancient Zoroastrian goddess who protects cattle, children, and friendship. The fourteenth day of the month is dedicated to her.

Gandarewa: A Zoroastrian water-demon who continually tries to devour the good things of creation.

Geus-Tasan: In ancient Zoroastrian myth, Geus-Tasan is the divine creator of cattle.

Geus-Urvan: The old-Zoroastrian guardian of cattle. His name means 'soul of the ox.' He is the servant of Vohu Manah.

Hvarekhshaeta: In Zoroastrian mythology, the many-horsed sun god.

Indar: The old Zoroastrian god of warfare, courage and bravery.

Indra: Indra is one of the seven Daevas and the personification of apostasy. His eternal opponent is Asha vahishta.

Izha: The Indo-Zoroastrian goddess of the sacrifice.

Mah: An ancient Zoroastrian god of the moon, one of the Yazatas. He is associated with the cow, which plays an important part in old-Zoroastrian mythology, and presides over time and tide. He is mentioned as an assistant of Vohu Manah. The seventh day of the month is dedicated to Mah.

Mao: A Zoroastrian moon god.

Nanghaithya: One of the Daevas, and archfiend. Nanghaithya is the personification of discontentment. Her eternal opponent is Armaiti.

Neriosang: A Messenger-god in Zoroastrian mythology.

Peris: Zoroastrian spirits of great beauty who guide mortals on their way to the Land of the Blessed. They also battle the Daevas.

Rapithwin: The ancient Zoroastrian god of midday, the protecting deity of the south and of summer.

Saurva: Saurva is one of the seven main Daevas. His eternal opponent is Khshathra vairya.

Sraosa: Sraosa is a member of the Amesha Spentas. He is the personification of obedience and the messenger of the great god Ahura Mazda. He also guides the souls of the deceased to find their way to the after live. His symbolic animal is the cock, whose crowing will call the pious to their religious duties. The seventeenth day of the month is dedicated to him. His eternal opponent is the archdemon Aesma Daeva.

Srosh: In middle Zoroastrian myths the messenger of the gods. He was sent down from heaven to announce to a king that his last hour had struck.

Vanant: In Zoroastrian mythology, one of the four leaders of the stars that fight for Ahura Mazda; the guardian star of the west who conquers evil.

Verethragna: The Zoroastrian god of victory and the personification of aggressive triumph. God of Vrahran Fire, the most sacred of all fires. It is a combination of 16 fires, most of which belong to those in the metal trades. He punishes the evil done by man and demon. Verethragna appears in many shapes: bear, bird of prey, bull, camel, youth, warrior with a golden sword, wind, etc. His appearance as a bird and bear were especially popular. The twentieth day of the month is dedicated to him.

Vouruskasha: The world ocean in Zoroastrian cosmology; it is also the sea deity. A heavenly lake that supplies water to the world and in the middle of which grows the Tree of Life.

Zam: In old-Zoroastrian (Avestan) mythology, Zam is the deified earth. He is one of the Yazata.

Zam-Armatay: The Zoroastrian goddess of the earth.

Zarich: Zarich is one of the female members of the Daevas and the personification of ageing. Her eternal opponent is Ameretat.

Zrvan Akarana: The primordial god in Zoroastrian religion, and the god of infinite time and space. He is the father of the good god Ahura Mazda and the evil god Angra Mainyu. With children representing the two opposites, Zrvan Akarana himself is regarded as a neutral god; one for whom there is no distinction between good or evil. Zrvan Akarana is also the god of destiny, light and darkness.

Amesha Spentas, Fravashis and the Yazatas

Other than these Gods and Demons, special attention was given to the presence of Fravashis who were equal to the Archangels of Christianity. The word Fravashis literally means 'Guardian Angels.' Zoroastrianism recognizes various classes of spiritual beings besides the Supreme Being (Ahura Mazda): The Amesha Spentas, Yazatas, and Fravashis.

1. Amesha Spentas 'the Archangels': Literally, 'Beneficent Immortals,' these are the highest spiritual beings created by Ahura Mazda. The Amesha Spentas ('beneficent immortals'), come directly after him in the hierarchy of gods, and can be compared with archangels. They are gods without being gods and creatures without being creatures. Together they fight for truth and justice. Their names are:

Vohu Mano: lit. Good Mind. Presides over cattle. Vohu Manah is one of the Amesha Spentas, and the personification of wisdom. He is the protector of the animal world and is on earth represented by beneficial animals, especially the cow. He takes the souls of the just to Paradise. The eleventh month is dedicated to him. His eternal opponent is the archdemon Aka Manah.

Asha Vahishta: Highest Asha, the Amahraspand presiding over Asha and fire. Asha vahishta ('excellent order') is the personification of the 'best truth' and protects the physical and moral order on earth. He is the most prominent of the (male) Amesha Spentas and the principal adversary of the world of the demons. The second month is dedicated to him. His eternal opponents are the arch demon of lie, Drug and the archdemon of apostasy, Indra.

Khshathra Vairya: lit. 'Desirable Dominion,' the Amahraspand presiding over metals. One of the Amesha Spentas, Khshathra vairya is the personification of desirable dominion and is associated with metal. He is the protector of the poor even though he would rather defend royalty. He enforces peace by using his weapons. His attributes are the helmet, the shield and the spear. The sixth month is dedicated to him. His eternal opponent is the archdemon Saurva.

Spenta Armaiti: lit. 'Holy Devotion,' the Amahraspand presiding over the earth. In ancient Zoroastrian mythology, Spenta Mainyu ('holy spirit') is the god of life and the personification of the good and the light. He is the twin brother of Angra Mainyu (Ahriman), the god of darkness, with whom he fights an eternal battle.

Haurvatat: lit. 'Perfection or Health.' Presides over water. Haurvatat ('wholeness') is one of the seven Amesha Spentas. She is the personification of perfection and is associated with life after death. She brings prosperity and health. The third month is dedicated to her. Her eternal opponent is the archdemon of hunger, Tawrich.

Ameretat: lit. 'Immortality,' the Amahraspand presiding over the Earth. One of the Amesha Spentas, Ameretat is the personification of immortality and the protector of plants. The fifth month is dedicated to her. Her eternal opponent is the arch demon of ageing, Zarich.

Armaiti: She is one of the Amesha Spentas. She is the personification of holy devotion, the daughter of the creator and represents righteous obedience. She is associated with the earth and in that capacity she is the goddess of fertility and the dead, who are buried in the earth. The fifth day of every month and the twelfth month are dedicated to her. Her eternal opponent is the archdemon of discontent, Nanghaithya.

2. Fravashis 'the Holy Guardian Angels': It is said that each person is accompanied by a guardian angel, which acts as a guide throughout one's life. They originally patrolled the boundaries of the ramparts of heaven, but volunteer to descend to earth to stand by individuals to the end of their days. They guide the souls of the deceased to heaven. Each family or clan has its own spirit that guards and only looks after. The Fravashis assisted Ahura Mazda in the creation of the world and, as riders armed with spears, are the defenders of heaven.

Legend says that Ahura Mazda advised Zarathushtra to invoke them for help whenever he found himself in danger. If not for their guardianship, animals and people could not have continued to exist, because the wicked Druj would have destroyed them all.

The Fravashi also serves as an ideal that the soul has to strive for and emulate. They manifest the energy of God, and preserve order in the creation. They are said to fly like winged birds, and are represented by a winged disk, often with a person superimposed.

3. Yazatas 'the Angels': lit. 'Adorable ones,' a created spiritual being, worthy of being honoured or praised. Like the Amesha Spentas they personify abstract ideas and virtues, or concrete objects of nature. The Yazatas are ever trying to help people, and protecting them from evil. In Zoroastrianism the Yazatas are the deities to whom the hymns in the Zend-Avesta are addressed. They are also the guardians of the celestial bodies and the messengers of Ahura Mazda. The chief Yazata is Mithra and some of the others include Daena, Mah, Rashnu, Tistrya, and Zam. Below is a list of the more important Yazatas.

Ahurani: Female Yazads presiding over water.

Airyaman: Yazad of friendship and healing. (Indo-Iranian in origin)

Akhshti: Yazad personifying peace.

Anaghra Raocha: Yazad of the 'endless light.'

Apam Napat: Yazad of waters (Indo-Iranian in origin).

Aredvi Sura Anahita: lit. 'Strong, immaculate Anahita,' female Yazad personifying water. She resides in the starry regions. Her hymn is preserved in Yasht 5. Also known as Aban Yazad.

Arshtat: Female Yazad personifying rectitude or justice.

Ashi Vanghuhi: lit. 'Good blessings, rewards,' female Yazad presiding over blessings.

Asman: Yazad presiding over the sky.

Atar: lit. Fire, the yazad presiding over fire, he is referred to as 'the Son of Ahura Mazda' in the Avesta.

Chisti: Female Yazad personifying religious wisdom. Her name probably means 'Instruction.' Also known as Razishta Chista ('Most Upright Chista').

Daena: Female Yazad presiding over the religion, also, Inner Self or Conscience.

Dahm: Yazad honoured on the fourth day after death.

Dahma Afriti: embodiment of power of benediction.

Damoish Upamana: Yazad personifying anathema.

Drvaspa: Female Yazad personifying cattle.

Erethe: Female Yazad personifying truth.

Gaw: Yazad personifying cattle.

Geush Urvan: lit. 'The soul of the cow (or settlement).' Personification of all animal life.

Haoma: Yazad presiding over the haoma plant, which has medicinal and spiritual properties. (Indo-Iranian in origin)

Haptoiringa: A star Yazad, associated with Ursa Major.

Havani: Yazad presiding over the second watch (gah) of each day. (Sunrise to midday, i.e., at 12 noon.)

Hvare-khshaeta: lit. 'The shining sun,' the Yazad presiding over the Sun.

Khwarenah: Yazad presiding over Divine Grace or Fortune.

Maonghah: Yazad presiding over the Moon.

Manthra Spenta: lit. 'Holy Word,' Yazad who embodies the Holy Word.

Mithra: Yazad presiding over the contract, personification of light. (Indo-Iranian in origin)

Nairyosangha: Yazad who acts as messenger of Ahura Mazda, associated with prayer. (Indo-Iranian in origin)

Paoiryaenis: Star Yazad associated with the Pleiades.

Parendi: Female Yazad of 'Abundance' or 'Plenitude.' (Indo-Iranian in origin)

Paurwanya: Star Yazad associated with a constellation of uncertain identity.

Raman: Yazad presiding over Joy or Felicity.

Rapithwin: Yazad presiding over the period of the day (gah) from noon to mid-afternoon.

Rasanstat: Female Yazad personifying truth.

Rashnu: The Zoroastrian divine angel of justice and last judgement and the personification of righteousness. Along with Mithra and Sraosa he judges the souls of the dead. Rashnu guards the Chinvat Bridge leading to heaven. He carries the golden scales with which he weighs the souls at Judgement.

Rata: Female Yazad (Indo-Iranian in origin) personifying charity.

Satavaesa: A star Yazad, perhaps of Fomalhaut.

Sraosha: lit. 'Hearkening', a spirit being who guards the soul for three days after death.

Thwasha: Personification of 'Infinite Space.'

Tishtrya: Yazad presiding over the star Sirius. Tishtrya also directs the rain.

Tishtryaeinis: Star Yazad associated with Canis Minor.

Ushah: Female Yazad of the dawn. (Indo-Iranian in origin)

Ushahin: Yazad presiding over the first watch (gah) of each day (from midnight to daybreak).

Uzerin: Yazad presiding over the fourth watch (gah) of each day (from 3 p.m. to sunset).

Vanant: Star Yazad, associated with Vega.

Vata: The ancient Zoroastrian god of the wind and one of the Yazatas. The twentieth day of the month is dedicated to him.

Vayu: Yazad personifying the wind or atmosphere. (Indo-Iranian in origin)

Verethraghna: lit. 'Victory', Yazad personifying victory. (Indo-Iranian in origin)

Visya: Yazad associated with the settlement, invoked along with Savanghi.

Zamyat (Zam): Female Yazad presiding over the earth.

Zantuma: Yazad presiding over the tribe.

Zrvan Akarana: Personification of 'Boundless Time.'

Religious ceremonies and rituals

Since the Persians came to India, they have been affected by the traditions of this Hindu land. The Zoroastrians have adopted the language, the dress and a part of the marriage ceremony from the people of India. There are a large number of minor ceremonies and superstitions that have entered into their daily life in the course of the many centuries that they have lived in this country. Still, on the whole, the Zoroastrian community has kept up its ancient tradition and has maintained an individual existence, even though in actual numbers they seem seldom to have exceeded some hundred thousand in India. Having lived in India now for over eleven centuries, and having adopted the language and the dress of the land, they have outwardly merged into the Indian people forming but one of the many communities of the country. But on the most important occasions of human life-initiation, marriage and death, they clearly show their individual existence as a separate community, distinctly different from the other races of India. Here is the description of some of the most important ceremonies that form an integral part of people following Zoroastrianism.

1. The Boi Ceremony

The 'Boi Machi' Ceremony accompanies the worshipping of the fires, five times each day. During this ceremony sandalwood is burned, because of its sweet fragrance. The Priest then says certain prayers, and then on the fire he places six pieces of both sandalwood and incense. The wood is put in an 'adafargan, or fire urn, carrying a metal ladle, the priest circles the fire, stopping eight times to say prayers. The priest then hits a bell, and calls for the Holy Spirit to be present in the room. Then the ceremony comes to a close. After the ceremony, the priest uses the ladle to give ashes from the fire to all the worshippers present there.

2. The Holy Days

The followers of Zoroastrianism do not gather weekly for a worship service. Instead, they recite their basic prayers five times each day, whether they are alone or with a group. People who believe in Zoroastrianism have holidays and festivals when they get together for worship and celebration.

There are seven major Zoroastrian festivals each year. These are the 'holy days' when the rich and the poor come together to feast, with each person contributing as much as they are able to.

Six Gahambars	English Name	Associated Immortal
1. Maidhyoizaremaya	Midspring	Khshathra
2. Maidhyoishema	Midsummer	Haurvatat
3. Paitshahya	Harvest	Spenta Armaity
4. Ayathrima	Bringing in Cattle	Ameratat
5. Maidhyairya	Midwinter	Vohu Mana
6. Hamaspathmaedaya Muktad	All Souls	Spenta Mainyu / Ahura Mazda
7. NoRoz	New Year	Asha Vahista

Associated Creation	Time of Year
1. Sky	April/May
2. Water	June/July
3. Earth	September
4. Plants	October
5. Cattle	January
6. Humans	March
7. Fire	March

The seventh and highest festival of the year is NoRoz (New Year). NoRoz celebrates the creation of fire and the Immortal Asha Vahista, or highest truth. NoRoz is the most sacred and joyous religious ceremony of all. It represents the renewal of life in the spring, and it also represents the new order to come with Frashogard (world renewal). During this time of year, people give gifts, wear new clothes, settle arguments and visit their fire temples to re-affirm their faith.

3. Jashan

Jashan is the Thanksgiving and Memorial Ceremony of the Zoroastrian people. It is usually preformed between the last Gahambar and NoRoz. But it may be preformed anytime if someone wants to express gratitude and happiness. Jashan requires at least two priests, but often four take part. It represents a dialogue between spiritual and physical worlds. It invites Ahura Mazda, the Amesha Spentas, the Yazates, the Fravishes and the souls of the deceased to join in. The priest then feeds the fire with sandalwood and incense, and says some special prayers. A great feast always accompanies the Jashan ceremony for all the community.

4. Navjote

Navjote is the ceremony when the children are initiated into Zoroastrianism. This ceremony takes place before puberty between the ages of seven and nine for both boys and girls. But before anyone could be initiated, they must learn the ways of Zoroastrianism. So, the Zoroastrian parents teach their children right from the birth. The Navjote ceremony is the same for both genders, with no special rules or regulations. It is the first time that the child wears the 'armour of the religion': the sudrah (shirt) and kusti, which should then be worn every day for the rest of his/her life. The initiate goes through other certain preparations for the ceremony. During the ceremony, special prayers and sayings are said, and then the initiate gets blessed.

The sudrah (shirt) that is to be worn next to the skin is made of white cotton, usually thin muslin. With white being a symbol of stainlessness and purity to remind the wearer that his/her deeds must be as pure and spotless as the sacred shirt they are wearing. The sudrah is made up of two pieces of cloth sewn together on the sides; the two parts, the back and the front symbolic of the past and future, both related to each other through the present. In the front, over the chest is a small pocket (girehban). This is called the pocket of righteousness; it is the symbolic collection place for the wearer's good words, good thoughts and good deeds.

The kusti is woven out of white lamb's wool, and the process of weaving it is a complex one. Only women of the priestly class weave it. For that first of all the wool is spun into a fine thread and two threads of the requisite length are twisted together, symbolising the union of the Two Spirits for manifestation. Then seventy-two such double strands are taken and woven together into a long thin hollow tape. The number seventy-two represents the seventy-two chapters of the Yasna, the most important book of the Scriptures. The hollow tape is then turned carefully inside out after which there is a ceremonial washing and finally it is rolled up tightly. Every detail in the preparation of the kusti is symbolical as the seventy-two strands are also divided into six groups of twelve each, these numbers also having definite significance.

As worn over the sudrah, the kusti goes round the waist thrice, to signify the three commandments of Zoroaster – the humata, the hukhta, and the huvarshta. It is secured by 'a sailor's knot' before and behind. Each twist of these knots is meant to bring one important truth to the mind of the wearer: (1) God is the One Eternal Being, (2) The Zoroastrian Faith is the true Faith, (3) Zoroaster is the true inspired Prophet of God, and (4) The wearer shall try to obey the three commandments. The untying and retying of the kusti, accompanied by the kusti prayers, is always done facing the direction of a source of light: the sun, the moon or a lamp. Along with the sudrah, the kusti is the 'badge' of all believers, male or female, rich or poor, priest or layman.

Although the Navjote ceremony is short in length, it still remains mandatory and infused with heavy symbolism to the extent that it may be considered as one of the most important events in a Zoroastrian's life. During this ceremony, the child receives its first ceremonial bath, the Nahn; the opening prayer (Patet) is said, followed by a Confession of Faith and a central penitential prayer (Nirang-i-kusti). Then there are two traditional chants (Ahuna Vairya and Ashem Vohu), the Articles of Faith, and the final Benediction.

The Zoroastrian have kept up this ancient attire almost unchanged for centuries. But among the Hindus the shirt had dwindled down to a mere thread – Janeu or Yagyopavit - the sacred thread worn across the chest and over the left shoulder, while the girdle, though worn at the time of the investiture, has dropped out almost completely. Zoroastrians believe that children cannot tell the difference between right and wrong, and therefore cannot sin. Once children freely choose to be initiated, they become adults responsible for their own thoughts, words, deeds, which determines the fate of their souls on judgment day.

5. Weddings

All Aryans have always regarded the state of matrimony as the most important part of life. In the religious scripture, 'Vendidad' it is clearly indicated that Ahura Mazda is better pleased with a married man than with an unmarried one. Therefore, it has always been regarded as the bounden duty of the Zoroastrian to marry and to bring up a family, and thus to ensure the continuance of the race and the religion. This concept totally matches with that of the Hindus as also stated in 'Manusmriti,' the Hindu law book.

When the Zoroastrians first landed at Sanjan in Gujarat, and asked for the permission of the Yadava Prince of that land to settle down in his territory, they were asked to change their time of marriage ceremony. The time for the celebration was thus changed from daylight to immediately after sunset. The essential part of the ceremony consists of the recital three times of the marriage contract by the officiating priest. The original formula is in the Pahlavi language, which was the language of Iran at the time of the Arab conquest. The same ceremony is often repeated in Sanskrit as well, out of deference to a promise given to the Yadava Prince that the marriage ceremony should also be conducted in a language known to the rulers of the land where they had been permitted to settle down.

The essential part of conversation at the time of the marriage ceremony is as follows:

The Priest: 'In the presence of this assembly, that has met together in... city, on the... day of month of in the year... of the Emperor Yazdegard Shahriar of the Sasanian dynasty of auspicious Iran say whether you have agreed to take this maiden named... in marriage for this bridegroom in accordance with the rites and customs of the Mazda worshippers, promising to pay her 2,000 dirhems of pure white silver and two dinars of standard gold of Nishahpur coinage'?'

The Witness of Bridegroom: 'I have.'

The Priest: 'And have you and your family with pure mind and truthful thoughts, words and deeds and for the increase of righteousness, agreed to give for ever and aye, this bride in marriage to...?'

The Witness of Bridegroom: 'I have agreed.'

The Priest: 'Have you desired to enter into this contract with pure mind and until Death do ye part?'

The Witness of Bridegroom: 'I have so desired.'

The rest of the ceremony is the invocation of the blessings of God and of the Amesha-Spentas and of the Yazatas upon the newly joined couple and an address from the Priest to them as to their conduct in life.

Thus, Zoroastrian weddings are a lot like that of the Hindus. The priest blesses the couple, and then the couple declares their vows to each other. After the vows are said, the people attending the ceremony bless the couple and immediately after that, they are showered with rice. Rice is considered to be a symbol of prosperity and joy.

Though the Zoroastrians have adopted European costume and they go about bare headed most of the time, still at times of prayers, inside the temples and during all religious ceremonies the wearing of small velvet or silken skullcap is compulsory. Orthodox and old fashioned women tie up their hair with a white cotton kerchief, so as to have the head always covered, and even though today kerchief has been discarded, still at prayer time their head must be covered either with the kerchief or with their silk sari. Among the Hindus the tuft of hair worn on the top of the head by the men, 'the Shikha' corresponds in its original object with the cap of the Zoroastrians.

In every important ceremony, such as the seasonal festivals, thanksgiving ceremonies, death anniversaries, etc., the great ancestors are invoked and remembered by their name. All the heroes of ancient Iran as well as all those who have served the community since the migration of the Zoroastrians into India are remembered with gratitude. To have one's name included in this list is the highest honour that a Zoroastrian may attain in his life. There is a general list that is used by Zoroastrians all over India on such occasions, and each town has besides its own local list. Though the dead have no monuments erected to their memory, they have something far more glorious than any stone structure could be and it is the loving remembrance of their fellow men, which they had served.

Praying

Prayer comprises the most important part of the Zoroastrian daily life. Each sunrise comes with a prayer and each sunset ends in a prayer. There are numerous prayers found in the holy scriptures of the Zoroastrians that are said on respective occasions. These prayers show the reverence, faith and thankfulness that the community has in its heart for the Supreme Gods and Angels. In the common prayers of the Zoroastrians, it can be seen that Ahura Mazda is considered the Supreme Being, the giver of happiness, the eliminator of evil and he is called by several names that are epithets to his holy image. While the prayer for Mithra, quite astonishingly comprises the same thought flow as in the Vedas.

Fire worship

Zoroastrianism, much like many other religions, places a heavy emphasis on traditional rituals. Even today the strength of ritual is considered to be a prominent part of modern day Zoroastrianism, and among these rituals, the most important is the nourishment of the perpetual flame in the holy shrines. Legend says that the great fires have been burning since ancient prehistoric time. It is believed that the first fire was brought from heaven on the back of the mythical ox, Srishok, with a purpose to guide and protect all humanity.

Fire represents spiritual dominance of light over darkness and as such good over evil. It is considered as the ultimate symbol of Ahura Mazda. It still holds its significance in being a precious and sacred element representing the continuing presence of Ahura

Mazda. It gives light, warmth and energy to the other six creations, and so creates life. All the religious rituals are solemnized in the presence of fire, the life-energy. Hence, in Zoroastrian shrines, the ritual flame is never allowed to flicker out of existence. The flame carries such importance that the physical structure of the temple centres on it, maintaining its life. Due to this sacredness of the flame, common people are not allowed to fuel it. The fire remains dependant upon the priests for its life, priests who constantly purify themselves in order not to contaminate it. There is even a use of a covering for the mouth and nose to prevent the priest's exhaled breath or saliva from making the sacred fire impure. Even the presence of a non-Zoroastrian in a consecrated place (such as the location of the fire or even the temple itself) is regarded as a contamination. The rituals for purifying fires are preformed 1128 times in a year. The most sacred fires are in the temples in Iran and India, and they have been burning constantly for centuries.

This same concern for purity is found everywhere in Zoroastrianism. It was once custom to keep a ritual flame burning in the home of a pregnant woman, though in the present day the more common practice is to light a lamp after the fifth and seventh weeks of pregnancy. The purity rules of most importance are those pertaining to the birth itself and the confinement of the mother afterward. The delivery room is consecrated, and a light is burnt for three or more days in the confinement room as a protection from evil forces. The mother stays isolated in the confinement room for forty days, unable to contaminate others through contact with the regular living quarters. The confinement is concluded with a ritual bath for which a priest and consecrated water are required.

The Zoroastrians even do not leave their head uncovered and do not smoke. But there are no caste divisions, no religious restrictions about food. Their worship of fire is the highest and purest symbol of the Divinity. The Zoroastrians have remained faithful to their Zoroastrian faith and are proud of their racial purity. Marriage with outsiders is rare.

There are eight Atash Behrams, or Victorious Fires in India. Four are in Mumbai, four in the State of Gujarat, two in Surat, and the remaining in Udwada and Navsari. The Iranshah Atash Behram at Udwada is the oldest (720 AD). Here is the original fire brought by the fleeing Zoroastrians from Iran and consecrated shortly after their arrival at Sanjan, India. The village of Udwada is hence considered as a centre of pilgrimage by the Zoroastrians and is visited by thousands every year.

Ancestral worship

Prayers for the departed form an important part of the Zoroastrian ritual. Death anniversaries of every relative are carefully observed. The ceremony involves one important ritual and that is the invocation of the Fravashis of the departed. The idea of the Fravashis is somewhat similar to that of the Pitris among the Hindus but with a difference. The Fravashi is the highest and the eternal principle in a human being. Zoroastrians believe that not only humans but also all creatures possess their own Fravashis even plants have one. They are considered to persist through all eternity. It is said that they have existed since the beginning of creation and will go on till the end. They also seem to progress continually from one state to another higher and holier sphere. The Yazatas and the

Amesha-Spentas also have their Fravashis. Even Ahura Mazda has his Fravashi. The Zoroastrians only invoke the Fravashis of the good, for they are regarded as the guardians of creation, and they help all pious people in all their good work and bless every effort of progress and righteousness.

Death rituals

Death and the ceremonies that follow it always form the most important and the most impressive part of ritual in almost every ancient religion. Among the Zoroastrians it even starts with the person being on deathbed. At such a moment, to chant the sacred verses of Ashem Vohu and Ahuna Vairya into the ears of the dying person is considered the foremost duty of the nearest relatives. The person dying if conscious is also required to join in these prayers.

Soon after the spirit has departed, the body is bathed and dressed in old worn out garments of white cotton. After that the nearest male relative puts on the sudreh and the kusti while reciting the appropriate prayers simultaneously. Then the entire body is covered with a long white robe in such a way that only the face and the ears are exposed open. Then a room in the house is washed and in a corner, some slabs of stone are laid for the body to rest upon. The body is to be carried for disposal in the daylight hours and the usual time for the funeral is either in the morning or in the afternoon. But as long as the body remains in the house a priest sits near reciting prayers, and keeping a fire burning with incense and sandalwood. None but the two Naseh-salars (corpse-bearers) can henceforth touch the body, and none may approach within three paces of the dead.

The Towers of Silence

As soon as the breath left the body, the corpse is regarded as impure. It was now to begin to decay and fall to pieces. Therefore it has to be destroyed as soon as possible and in such a manner that may be the least harmful to other living beings. Zoroastrians say that the dead matter soon becomes a centre of corruption and hence while disposing it care has to be taken so that none of the pure Elements created by Ahura Mazda are contaminated. That's why the Zoroastrians are enjoined 'to expose the dead body to the Sun.' Hence the body is not to be burnt, neither it is to be buried, nor thrown into water.

For this purpose, the structures known as the 'Towers of Silence' are erected. At the time when the corpse is to be carried for funeral, two Naseh-salars come in with an iron bier, and two priests stand at the door of the room facing the departed and reciting aloud the Ahunavaiti Gatha. After the reciting is over, the assembled friends and relatives take the last leave of the departed, bowing low before the dead. Then the bier is covered over with a white sheet and carried out. There are other men to help the two 'corpse-bearers', but these may not touch anything except the long handles of the bier. It may also be noted that the carriers of the body, the priests who say the prayers and the friends who follow up to the Tower of Silence, must be dressed in white, and they must always go in pairs, holding a white handkerchief between them. The colour of the dress indicates Purity and the going in pairs symbolises mutual help in the hour of sorrow.

Arriving at the Tower the procession halts at a certain distance from it, the bier is laid down, and the face is exposed for the last time. All assembled persons of the community bow low for the last salutation; and then the two 'corpse-bearers' carry the bier into the Tower. There the body is placed within its proper ring and denuded of all its clothing. The Zoroastrians believe that as they were naked to born into the world so they should depart naked too.

The Towers of Silence are of a cylindrical shape, about 20 to 30 feet high, enclosed all round by a thick wall and open to the sky. The only entrance left is an iron gate located at the eastern side of the wall, which is kept securely locked. Inside the Tower is a platform of solid masonry divided into three concentric rings, and right in the middle is a deep circular pit going down into the earth right up to the foundations. This pit also is constructed of solid masonry. The inner platform is made to slope towards the central pit. In each of the three concentric rings shallow depressions of three different sizes are arranged. The outermost ring contains the largest of these and they are meant to receive the bodies of men, the middle ring has somewhat smaller depressions, which are meant for women, and the innermost ring contains the smallest sized depressions and these are meant for the bodies of children. Between these three rings there are narrow raised ledges running all round, separating them one from the other; and these serve as paths along which any part of the interior may be approached without stepping over the bodies already exposed there.

The Tower of Silence, being open at the top, gives free access to birds of prey, vultures, etc. to devour dead bodies. The Magi probably introduced this mode of the disposal of the dead into Zoroastrianism during the ancient times. This practice is also a lively example of the Zoroastrian virtue of charity even after death by feeding the birds with cast-off bodies. In towns where there is a considerable Zoroastrian population such birds are encouraged to build their nests in the vicinity of the Towers. After the birds finish off the flesh, the bones are completely bleached by the sun and the air within a few days. These are then collected together and deposited within the central pit, where they crumble to dust. Thus rich and poor, saint and sinner, man, woman and child all find the same status at the long last and mingle with the dust together. No monument is erected to mark out the rich from the poor even after death.

The rains wash out the Tower and the water running into the pit is filtered through the bone dust there and through the filter beds, and through the four channels it reaches the soil. There are also narrow channels connecting each of the depressions with the central pit, along which all fluids ultimately drain into it. The bottom of the central pit is covered over with layers of sand and charcoal so as to make it a perfect filter; and this is also connected to four underground channels, which also contain filter beds. These channels ultimately lead deep down into the soil, and thus all fluids that ultimately enter the soil are thoroughly filtered and rendered harmless.

After death beliefs

Zoroastrianism regards the Soul as more important than the body. So, a lot of attention is given to the rituals that may lead the soul to heaven. The scriptures give a very vivid description of the whole so-called journey of the soul. It is said that on the morning of the fourth day after the departure of the soul from the dead body, it crosses over the Chinvat-bridge where the good are separated from the bad.

Fate of a good soul

As exactly translated from the religious scripture, the account goes as:

And when the soul of the saved passes over that bridge, the bridge appears to it to be one broad; and the soul of the saved passes on accompanied by the blessed Sraosha. And his own good deeds come to meet him in the form of a maiden who is more beautiful and fair than any girl on the earth. And the soul of the saved asks in curiosity, "Who are you? I had never seen on earth a maiden more beautiful and fair than you." Then the maiden answers, "I am no maiden, but your own good deeds, young sir, whose thoughts, words, deeds, and religion are all good. For when on earth you saw one who offered sacrifice to the demons, then you sat apart and offered sacrifice to the gods. And when you saw a man commit violence, hurting good men then you helped people recover from that stat, you were good for the community, and you always welcomed people and offer them hospitality and give alms to the needy. You accumulated wealth with righteousness. And when you saw someone who passed false judgement, taking bribes and bore false witness, then spoke witness right and true. I am all such good thoughts, good words, and good deeds that you ever did or spoke. Though I was honourable, you made me yet more honourable; and though I was endowed with dignity, you conferred on me yet greater dignity."

And when the soul departs from there, then it senses the blowing of a fragrant breeze towards it, more fragrant than any perfume on earth. Then the soul founds itself standing in front of Sraosha and asks, "This kind of fragrance I have never smelled on earth, what is this?" Then the blessed deity Sraosha answers to the soul of the saved, "This is a breeze from heaven; hence is it so fragrant." Then with its first step the soul treads the heaven of good thoughts, with its second the heaven of good words, with its third the heaven of good deeds; and with its fourth step it attains to the Endless Light where all is eternal bliss. And all the gods and the angels come to greet him. Then they serve him with the sweetest of foods, even the butter of early spring, so that the soul may take its ease after the spending of the three nights of terror at the Bridge which the other demons brought upon him; and then he is given a throne to sit. And as such forever and ever he dwells in a plenitude of bliss together with the spiritual gods.

The acquaintance with God is only one of the joys of heaven, though no doubt the greatest. After being introduced into the divine presence newly arrived soul is greeted by his friends, made welcome, and told of all the joys that await him there. The soul then enjoys the company of learned and pious friends and of wives who are fair and modest, devoted to the husbands. There is also present all the creatures of the animal kingdom, flocks and herds, wild animals, birds, and fish along with all the good forces of nature, fires and winds, shining metals, and water in rivers, springs, and wells. Despite this description, it is clear that the Zoroastrians regarded heaven as being a perfect place where personal relationships would subsist and sensuous pleasures would be enjoyed.

Fate of an evil soul

But when the man who is damned dies, then for three days and nights his soul hovers near his head, weeping and saying, "Where shall I go and in whom shall I now take refuge?" And during those three days and nights he sees with his eyes all the sins and wickedness that he had committed on earth. On the fourth day the demon Vizarsh comes and binds the soul of the damned in most shameful wise, and, despite the opposition of the blessed Sraosha, drags it off to the bridge. Then Rashnu, the judge, unmasks the soul of the damned as damned.

Then the demon Vizarsh, seizes upon the soul of the damned, smite it and despite it without pity. And the soul of the damned cries out with a loud voice, groans making a piteous plea; and desperate to break its bondage. When all his struggling and his lamentations have proved of no use, no help is proffered to him by any of the gods nor yet by any of the demons, but the demon Vizarsh drags him off against his will to the darkest hell.

Then a maiden who yet has no resemblance to a maiden comes to meet him. And the soul of the damned asks her, "Who are you for never have I seen an ill-favoured on earth more ill-favoured and hideous than you?" And in answer that ugly maiden says to him, "I am no girl, but I am your own deeds -hideous deeds- your evil thoughts, evil words, evil deeds, and evil religion. For when on earth you saw one who offered sacrifice to the gods, then you sat apart and offered sacrifice to the demons. And when you saw one who welcomed good men and offered them hospitality, and gave alms both to those who came from near and to those who came from far, then you treated good men with dishonour; you didn't give them alms, but shut your door upon them. And when you saw someone who passed just judgement, or took no bribes, or bore true witness, or spoke up in righteousness, then you sat down and passed false judgement and bore false witness. I am all those evil thoughts, evil words, and evil deeds that you ever thought and spoke and did. For though I was disreputable at first, you made me more disreputable; and though I was dishonourable at first, you made me more dishonourable."

Then with the first step the soul goes to the hell of evil thoughts, with his second to the hell of evil words, and with his third to the hell of evil deeds. And with his fourth step he is thrown into the company of the destructive spirit and other demons. And the demons mock at him, fearing him with various tortures. Then they bring him poison and venom, snakes and scorpions and other noxious reptiles that thrive in hell and give to him for eating. And until the resurrection and the final body he remains in hell suffering.

As such the Mithra and Rashnu are considered to be the great judges, while Sraosha watches over all of them. Hence the Judges give the departed the exact reward for all acts done during the earthly life.

Zoroastrianism, like Hinduism and Christianity, lays great stress on individual salvation; yet the fate of the individual is ultimately seen in the context of the whole of the human race. That's why the plan of Ohrmazd's plan to defeat Ahriman also has a hidden meaning; it is symbolic to the final release of all the souls of the damned from hell. In Sassanian Zoroastrianism there is no eternal damnation; no soul is eternally punished for the sins it has committed in time. So not only Ahriman and the demons are destroyed, but also the effects of evil and the sufferings endured by the damned in hell, all are destroyed. But before that joyful consummation each individual soul has to answer for itself and has to undergo an individual judgement after death. In this respect the Zoroastrianism of the Sassanian reform is true to the Prophet's message that each man much choose between good and evil and must bear the consequences of his choice. The judgement of the soul at death is still preserved in a fragment of the Avesta and frequently appears in the Pahlavi books.

The Nature of a Discarnate Soul

From the description of the soul's fate after death, it can be seen that the Zoroastrian conception of the nature of the soul is a bit materialistic. The soul seems to see, hear, touch, smell, and taste, and it has the equivalent of physical organs, for it eats. So as far as the scriptures are concerned, the soul is considered to be an unseen genius of the body. It has the same senses as the body through which it can enjoy the pleasures of paradise and suffer the torments of hell. Every soul which awaits judgement has to await on the bridge on the first three nights during which even the soul of the virtuous man suffers punishment for the few sins it has committed before it passes on to paradise. On the other hand, mythology explains that the soul of the wicked man who had done some virtuous deeds ever in his life, is visited by the spirit of good thoughts on the first night, by the spirit of good words on the second, and by the spirit of good deeds on the third thus bringing him some comfort to console him for what was going to fall on him – the pains of the hell.

Thus Hell is a kind of solitary confinement in a freezing and stinking darkness. It is laid out in three layers of descending gloom, situated in the north, between the underside of the earth and on that part of the sky that is below the earth. The sole companions of the evil souls are the demons that actually are the person's own evil deeds personified as demons to torment him. Despite the fact that these dead souls are fed on the most ill substances yet they are never satisfied and always crave for more.

Heaven and hell are not considered the same for all. Their joys and pains are strictly commensurate to the amount of virtue or sin a man has accumulated during his earthly life. The Zoroastrian scriptures even go further in explaining the fate of the soul of persons who had equal good and bad deeds. There is another place for such purposes; this is called Hamestagan, the 'place of the mixed', destined for those whose balance of virtue and sin is exactly equal. This is situated between earth and the stars, and the only pain the soul suffers there is from heat and cold.

Decline

The Sasanian Church was the main protector and promoter of Zoroastrianism, yet even the Church experienced ups and downs as it sometimes upheld the true spirit of Zoroastrianism, and at other times became dogmatic. The Pahlavi period also marked the division of Zoroastrianism into many sects, as a result of the Christian influences in Iran. But the Sasanian had been the last great Zoroastrian Empire; in 650 A.D., it fell at the hands of Arab Muslims. This event also marked the fall of Zoroastrianism as the official state religion, and many Zoroastrians were converted to Islam, and Zoroastrian scholarship diminished greatly.

In the period 910-950 A.D., the Zoroastrian migrated to India, escaping from the severe persecution in their homeland. The exiled Zoroastrianism became known as Parsis or Parsees, two variations on a word meaning Persians. The situation of the Zoroastrians who fled into India was better than for those who stayed behind in Iran. The Zoroastrians who stayed behind became the unenthusiastic remnants of a formerly strong religious community. While in India, although it took some centuries of hardship, Zoroastrians found prosperity and progress, became socially strong and more religious. Zoroastrian texts were translated into Sanskrit and Hindi and as such the overall scholarship thrived.

The result of contact with Indians and their religion had a notable effect on Zoroastrian belief and practice, especially in terms of Hindu Mysticism. Within Zoroastrianism grew up various schools of mysticism, as well as ascetic practices, both unknown to the earlier religion of Zoroaster. And this adoption of foreign elements is a fact of any religion that lasts long enough and gains a large geographic spread.

Orthodox Zoroastrianism continued to face challenges well into the 19th century through the hands of different missionaries who came to India to spread their religion by managing to shake the faith of many Zoroastrians in India by finding "holes" in Zoroastrian teachings and forming arguments against the religion based on them. Zoroastrians who had not had formal training in the religious texts found themselves helpless on the argument ground because they had been relying on faith and on a vast oral tradition.

Due to the Western education, travel and trading, the 20th century Zoroastrian community was influenced by greater contact with people and materials of other religions. Cults and other mystical influences took hold within mainline Zoroastrianism, and this also caused divisions within the faith. Today, Zoroastrianism finds itself getting challenged by a number of issues. The main concern is over the waning number of active practitioners.

The essence of this religion lies in the theory that good is symbolized by light, evil by darkness. So the destruction of evil and the sole sovereignty of the good can only mean that the material world is transformed into pure light.

Zoroastrians believe that the sun, moon, and stars will exist, but there will be no need for daylight or a succession of glimmering dawns, for the whole world will be light and devoid of any darkness, and each individual will be light. Being light, they will be full of joy. And all creatures will have but one will and one desire. Individual men will feel no envy at the joy of the totality of created things, but will rejoice together with it. The goodness and joy allotted to each will wax and grow in the glory of the omnipotence of him, Ahura Mazda, who is all-good, all-aware, all in all through his overflowing bounty and perfect skill in means.

****

CHAPTER-5

ESOTERICISM

The word 'esotericism,' like the adjective 'esoteric,' has different meanings in different contexts, and this is a major cause of confusion about the nature of this belief. In general, we can define this word in five different ways at instance. Firstly the word 'Esotericism' is commonly used as a synonym of 'the occult.' Secondly, the adjective 'esoteric' may be related to the secret teachings of a religion. Thirdly, the esoteric may be defined as a metaphysical concept emphasising on the unity of esoteric religions. Fourthly, in religious studies, it is also used as a synonym of gnosis in the universal sense of the world. Fifthly, on seeing through a historical perspective, esotericism is a mixture of interrelated concepts and traditions from the early modern period up to the present day. Therefore, in a word we can say that esotericism is the 'occult philosophy' of the Renaissance and its later developments like Alchemy, Parapsychology and Rosicrucian beliefs.

It is a well-known truth that religion, like everything else, begins with ideas and ends with myths. But in all myths the seed of the esoteric root from which they sprang, may be found. Even in the Christian religion the dogmas are founded to a large extent upon the ancient pagan teachings, and therefore ultimately upon the esoteric truths. Since the origin of humans and in all races of men, whether civilized or barbarian, there has been the presence of an intuition, an intimation, persistent and enduring. This intuition always attracts the attention of the sub conscious mind towards a doctrine that holds in it the secrets of nature. But this is available only to those who qualify on the grounds of the cosmic by becoming worthy depositaries of it. In early time, to the inventive genius of so-called 'primitive' man, the views and legends of the natural phenomena that had occurred, and those that had aroused fear in the mind, were thought to be the work of gods and demons. Running in a directly contrary direction is the teaching brought again to the world through Esotericism. It believes in the presence of a true wisdom teaching power that is open to all, and is still full and complete in it. It also consists of the phenomena of the Universe and a complete historical account of the origin, nature, and destiny of Man himself.

This secret doctrine is the universally diffused religion of the ancient and prehistoric world. The proofs of its diffusion, authentic records of its history that prove its character and presence in every land, together with the teaching of all its great adepts, exist to this very day. It is not a religion, nor is a new philosophy; it is as old as the thinking of man. Although the main body of the doctrine is found scattered throughout hundreds and thousands of Sanskrit manuscripts disfigured in their interpretations, and hundreds of them still awaiting to be translated and interpreted.

Origin of Esotericism

Legend says that this Wisdom-Religion, this Ancient Doctrine, this Esoteric System, this Esotericism was delivered to the first thoughtful humans by highly intelligent spiritual entities from superior spheres; and since then it has been passed down from Guardians to Guardians until our own time. The Guardians are those men who have been enlightened and are fully grown spiritually. It is also found that those Guardians have given out portions of this original and majestic system at various periods of time to different races in different parts of the world whenever humanity stood in need of some new extension of religious beliefs.

In short we can say that in the world, there has been a presence of a completely coherent and fully comprehensive system of religious philosophy, or of philosophical, scientific religion, which from time to time has been given out to man whenever the world needs a fuller revealing of spiritual truth. This likewise means that every one of the great world religions and every one of the great world philosophies issued originally from such Guardians, and that all such religions and philosophies in consequence, have, each one at its centre. Thus it may be concluded that there are three main sources from which the Truth about Life and Man, flows forth into the world:

1. The 'Revelation' delivered to humanity by beings from higher spheres, of glorious spiritual and intellectual capacities and power, who inspire and teach the youthful mankind, and who finally withdrew to their own spheres, leaving behind the highest and best of pupils, chosen from among selected individuals of the youthful humanity.

2. The Guardians and Deliverers of this Wisdom to mankind, whenever the time permits a new impulse of spiritual and intellectual teaching to be given to the world.

3. The esoteric meanings of the fundamental principles of the great world religions, all of which contain various aspects of the Truth about the Universe and Man, while having the same driving force at the centre.

History and Development

On studying the masterpieces of literary development of ancient Greece and of countries under the Roman Empire, one finds that the greatest men during many centuries have left it on record that there is indeed such an Esoteric System that was recognised by the name of 'the Mysteries' that was the most carefully guarded, considered most holy and was strictly restricted to those men and women who had proved themselves worthy depositaries of that holy trust, worthy to be the recipients of that original and most majestic system which the earth has ever known.

In India, 'the holy motherland of religions and philosophies,' also is found the same tradition, the same body of teachings in practice. The difference is that in India, it is still kept holy, secret and esoteric. Therefore in Greece and Rome it is called 'a Mystery,' not in the sense of something non-understandable but in the original ancient sense which the Greek word *mysterion* had: something kept for the mystics, those initiated in the Mystery-Schools, to study and to follow the supreme ethical guidance in life.

In India, all religious and philosophical teachings have been divided into two parts: one for the common people and the other for the Dwijas, i.e., the 'twice-born,' the initiated ones. This inner, secret, sacred, holy teaching is called *rahasya*, a Sanskrit word meaning esoteric doctrine or mystery. Examples of literary works in which such teachings were embodied are the Hindu Upanishads, *Upanishad* being a Sanskrit compound word meaning verbally 'according to the sitting down,' or 'following upon the sitting down.'

The figure is that of pupils who sit in Oriental style at the feet of the Teacher, who teaches them in secret and in strict privacy, and in forms and manners of expression that were later reduced to writings.

If the Sanskrit compound U*panishad* is further analysed, it is found to be composed of the prepositional particle '*upa*,' 'according to,' the prepositional particle '*ni*,' 'down,' and the verbal root '*sad*,' 'to sit,' which becomes '*shad*,' by the rules of Sanskrit grammar when preceded by the particle '*ni* ': the entire compound thus signifying 'following upon or according to the teachings which are received when we were sitting down at the feet of the teacher.'

The sages of olden times left on record, the inner teaching of the religions of the peoples among whom they lived. This inner teaching is the esoteric philosophy, the theosophy of that particular period. In India this theosophy is openly found in the Upanishads, discussed above, which are in actuality a part of the Vedic literary cycle. The word itself implies 'secret doctrine' or 'secret teachings.' From the Upanishads and from other parts of the Vedic literature, the ancient sages of India produced what is called today the Vedanta, a compound Sanskrit word meaning 'the end (or completion) of the Vedas,' symbolising the holy instruction in the final and most perfect exposition of the meaning of the Vedic tenets.

In ancient Greece there were various schools of mysteries, and the theosophy of ancient Greece was held very secret. It was taught by different teachers; to very carefully selected bodies of their disciples. One of such great teachers was Pythagoras; another was Plato; and this esoteric philosophy was clearly outlined and embodied, after the fall of the pagan religions. It represented the actual inner teachings of Pythagoras, Plato, and the inner sense of those mystical doctrines that passed in Greece under the name of the Orphic poems.

In Egypt, the reference of Esotericism is found very scantly in 'The Book of the Dead.' Of the theosophy of ancient Europe, we have a certain number of mystical writings such as the Scandinavian Eddas, and the Germanic books, which are represented in the sagas found written in the Old High German and in the Anglo-Saxon tongues. The theosophy of the Jews was embodied in what was later called the Kabala, which literally means, 'to receive.' Thus it means that it was the traditional doctrine handed down or received (according to the statements of the Kabala itself) through the prophets and the sages of the Jews. Which according to the legend is said to have been first taught by 'God Almighty to a select company of angels in Heaven.' A study of the doctrines contained in the Upanishads, in 'The Book of the Dead,' in the Paganism philosophy, in the Scandinavian Eddas, etc. shows that they have one common basis, one foundation, one common truth. Various men in various ages taught the same truth, using different words and different figures, different metaphors; but underneath always was the ancient doctrine, the secret wisdom of the Esoteric.

It should be well remembered that the ancient teachers spoke and thought and taught *anthropocentrically; which means* that they all insisted on following the psychological laws of the human mind and therefore taught in human figures of speech, often using quaint metaphors, very odd, and yet so instructive as figures of speech.

Every great Teacher or Seer who has publicly come into the outer world of men from the company of the hermits has founded an inner circle, an inner school and teaches to these disciples of inner school, in more open form than was given to the outer world, the solution of the riddles of the universe and of human life.

This similar thought is found in Bible in a saying of Jesus, "Unto you it is given to know the mysteries of the kingdom of God: but to others in parables: that seeing they might not see, and though hearing they might not understand."

People of every ancient civilization such as the Greeks, the Romans, the Hindus, the Zoroastrians, the Egyptians, the Babylonians, all used different tongues and different ways to communicate and express themselves. But in all of them the esoteric messages were identical. So the Esoteric Tradition is considered as the Mother of world's great religions and philosophies.

However, all such world-religions or world-philosophies do not give a clear idea of the secret teachings that are at the core. One religion may be found emphasising on one or more such fundamental principles; while the other may emphasise on some other totally excluding the reference of the first ones. The reason behind is that every religion or philosophy, having its own place and period in time, represents the various human minds that have developed its doctrines and have translated it to the world in this or that particular form. So at instance it may seem as if the theories are different but the root, the core and the gist is the same in all of them.

Theory and Doctrine

Man's mind is a mirror, so when it is clean and pure, it is capable of accurately reflecting the thoughts, the impulses, the inspirations, the intuitions, which spring up in the human spirit and finally manifest as doctrines or teachings of truth. On the contrary, when the mind is imperfectly developed or filled with mental and passionate images it cannot translate and transmit with accuracy and perfection. So Esotericism lays emphasis on the purity and clarity of thought to keep oneself open to the truth of the cosmic. The Esotericism believes in:

1. The **ABSOLUTE**; the 'Parbrahma' of the Vedantins or the one Reality, **SAT**, which is both Absolute Being and Non-Being.

2. The first manifestation, the impersonal, and, in philosophy, Logos, the precursor of

the 'manifested.' This is the 'First Cause,' the 'Unconscious' of European Pantheists.

3. Spirit-matter, **LIFE**; the 'Spirit of the Universe,' the Purusha and Prakriti, or the

second Logos.

4. Cosmic Ideation, **MAHAT** or Intelligence, the Universal World-Soul; the Cosmic, the basis of the intelligent operations in and of Nature, also called **MAHA-BUDDHI**.

The one reality and its dual aspects in the conditioned Universe are emphasised as follows:

It is further believed that the eternity of the universe is the playground of numberless universes continuously appearing and disappearing, called as the manifesting of the stars and the sparks of Eternity.

This second assertion is the absolute universality of that law of periodicity, of flux and reflux which physical science has observed and recorded in all departments of nature. An alternation such as that of Day and Night, Life and Death, Sleeping and Waking, is a common and universal fact that it is easy to comprehend that in it we see one of the absolutely fundamental laws of the universe.

The third principle is that no purely spiritual divine Soul can have an independent conscious existence before the spark that issued from the pure Essence of the Universal Sixth principle or the OVER-SOUL. The exact channel for that is that first it has to pass through every elemental form of the phenomenal world and then by acquiring individuality, first by natural impulse, and then by self-induced and self-devised efforts ascends through all the degrees of intelligence, from the lowest to the highest, from mineral and plant, up to the holiest archangel. This is why the Hindus believe that the Universe is Brahma it is in every atom of the universe, the six principles in Nature being all the outcome of the SEVENTH and ONE, the only one perfect, real and true in the Universe whether Cosmically or micro-cosmically.

In its absoluteness, the One Principle under its two aspects is sexless, unconditioned and eternal. When the radiation radiates in its turn, all its radiations are bound to become male and female principles in their lower aspects. After Pralaya, the destruction of all life, the first that re-awakes to active life is the, Father-Mother, the Spirit and Soul of Ether, or the plane on the surface of the Circle. Space is called the 'Mother' before its cosmic activity, and Father-Mother at the first stage of re-awakening. The Jewish Kabala also calls it the Father-Mother-Son triangle. But whereas in the Eastern doctrine, these are the Seventh Principle of the manifested Universe, or its Spirit-Soul-Intelligence the triad branching off and dividing into the seven cosmically and seven humanly principles. At this stage of the re-awakening of the Universe, the sacred symbolism represents it as a perfect Circle with the (root) point in the Centre. This sign is universal and is found in the Kabala also.

Esoteric philosophy teaches that everything lives and is conscious, but not that all life and consciousness is similar to those of human or even animal beings. Life is one form of existence manifesting in physical matter. This matter is the vehicle for the manifestation of soul on this plane of existence, and soul is the vehicle on a higher plane for the manifestation of spirit, and these three are a trinity of life. This idea of universal life is one of those ancient conceptions that had been at the root of all ancient religions.

If we suppose an immense circle as a representation of the boundless 'all', which of course is merely a representation for space and then place a point in its centre. This point represents the first germ of the cosmic life. This point also has its meaning in the sense of a cosmic seed. Now it is not one point only in the cosmos that springs into activity during the creation process, but innumerable such points, such seeds are present. The number is limitless, practically; and each one of such points represents an individual from the previous era of life. This point in the quasi-infinitude of a hierarchy, of a universe, is the beginning of that hierarchy, and it represents the god of that hierarchy. This god itself is a synthetic aggregation of several other gods, representing the different smaller forces of nature in the same way as man's body is an aggregation, a synthesis, of multitudinous less or inferior lives.

Now this god clothes itself in its aura sending forth the vital vibrations necessary for the growth of life and as such these vibrations form the clothing of god. Any such god naturally casts its own individuality into clothing – all seven degrees or states of it. Its individuality is its nature. This nature of an entity is its individuality and it is the same quality which makes a rose bring forth always a rose, and not a lily; and which makes a man bring forth always a man and not some other sort of entity; and also which makes a god a god and not a monad. This may be called as *self-generation, self-pouring out. T*he pouring out of that which is within and therefore it gets derived to its individual and own characteristic.

But with the course of time, this god sends forth its clothed vibrations that consist of less or inferior beings. As man clothes himself in physical flesh, so the god clothes itself in a garment or body of vibrations, and this garment or body is composed of divine atoms. These divine atoms are the monads as compared with the god. Similarly the germ, the seed, the point which now can be termed as monad is one of the almost infinite number of monads in each god, forming the clothing of each god, the garments of light, in which a god lives, which it has sent forth from itself during its outpouring of individual life.

It is believed that there is a presence of five elements in nature, that are responsible for the creation of all living and non-living things not only on this earth but also in the universe. But these five basic elements are not the same as the chemical, simple or compound elements. These elements have already been recognized at the origin of most cultures and can best be described in contemporary scientific terms, as the 'basic environmental elements.' It is because they have been observed and considered of great importance by all men in all cultures in one form or another.

Earth

This represents the solid matter from which all the food, all materials for shelter, clothing and utensils come directly or indirectly. Hence earth or soil and rocks are usually called Mother, or the one who feeds and carries her children whether alive or dead.

Water

This represents the liquid matter used for drinking, cooking and for extracting substances from solid matter. It is indispensable to preserve life but necessary also as a cleansing agent. Earth and Water are closely related.

Air

The gaseous matter necessary for respiration and combustion and for the production of light. The earth, water and air are the indissoluble trio without which there can be no life.

Fire

This is the transformer of matter into non-matter. It is the heat or energy that keeps everything on a move whether living or non-living.

Ether or Akasa

It is the non-matter or the void that is unexplainable, indescribable aspect of nature that pervades everything. Everything has an opposite and Ether is the opposite of matter. In a way Ether is similar to the magic that endows the Great Power with its magical power and gives birth to the unreal. The most ancient Aryan Gods are frequently invoked as Asura in the Rigveda, because they are induced with the ultimate magical powers that give them almost unlimited and infinite power.

These five environmental elements were first conceived from the observation of nature. In many cultures such as Hinduism, Buddhism and Jainism, they have retained their original characteristics while in other cultures they have acquired different forms. In ancient Greece, the original four elements were earth; water, air, fire and they were well defined and established by Aristotle (384-322 B.C.) who superimposed four qualities on them. These qualities were: earth - cold and dry, water - cold and wet, air - hot and wet and fire - hot and dry.

In the Aryan Vedas, it is believed that earth and sky are fixed and hold up by the golden embryo or golden germ or seed that marks the auspicious beginning of all created beings including living beings, infused with the life principle of golden sunlight. This golden embryo or golden germ or seed is said to be the giver of breath, power and vigour 'whose shadow is immortality or death.' It is said that, "the unnamed God, the initial seed gives protection and under its shadow life can be used well, giving immortality, or poorly spelling death. He became the ruler of living things, man and animals, mountains (solid matter) and water (liquids, sea, rivers) are his arms; he is the one who establishes the firmament and measures sky or air. Finally the fourth element is the energy that animates the universe and transforms the material into immaterial and vice versa. Fire, is not only the energy principle that governs the struggle for life, but also the energy of God himself and obviously of life that sustains the germ or seed that was carried by the mighty waters.

Legend of Origin of the Universe

Esotericism, due to its scientific approach has a totally different explanation of the origin of life. It is said that in the beginning, the eternal power was wrapped in its lightened robes and slept for seven eternities. There was no time because it too lay asleep in the infinite bosom of duration. The universal thought process was also not present there. Neither there were the seven blessings nor there were any causes of misery because there was no one to produce them or get affected by them. Darkness alone filled the cosmic, for all the elements had merged together and the seed had not awakened to set the running of the new wheel of life. The visible and the invisible all rested in one eternal non-being. Life pulsated unconsciously in the cosmic. But there was neither silence nor sound, as the time had not yet come for the embryo to swell. But then the last vibration from the seventh eternity thrilled through infinitude, the embryo swelled like expanding from within, like a lotus bud. The vibration swept along touching the whole universe, darkness breathed and radiated a ray of light that in turn fell on the golden embryo. Then the radiant essence became seven inside, seven outside, the embryo expanded its root that grew in the ocean of life. There was the root of life in every drop of the ocean of immortality and this ocean was in itself an ocean of light that was the source of heat, fire and motion. Now the embryo was light itself. It expanded when the breath of fire fell upon it and became more radiant when it cooled down, expanding and contracting through its own self and the atoms are finally hardened. Each part finally reflected the self-existent lord like a mirror and thus turned in to a world of existence.

Then one ray multiplied the smaller rays, preceding life form. Life survived the last atom of form. Through such countless rays proceeds the life ray like a thread through many jewels immortally. When this ray become two, the three fold appears and becomes one thread, the thread of emotion – the heart of man. This thread passes through the seven worlds consequently. When it passes through the first, the metal and stone are formed. Through the second, a plant is formed and when this plant when this goes through different mystical changes, an animal is born. With the combined attributes of these a human is born. Thus the light, the Supreme, the God, the eternal power is clothed in the souls of all living beings.

Religious Practices

There is a quest in every human heart, which cannot be appeased by anything. This is a quest for something more truely than ordinary human beings, a hunger for the real, a hunger for the sublime, a never-ending quest. It is the nostalgia of the soul, of the spirit-soul of man attracted towards the unknown. The source of this longing is the homesickness brought about by the memory of the spiritual abode, from where we have come and towards which we are now on our return journey. Humans unconsciously and intuitively see the vision on the mountaintops of the mystic East and every human heart feels this yearning, homesickness for the indescribable, for the immortal. Search for eternal peace has been never been compromised since man began looking at the stars and thinking of the mysteries of the universe. It has been a well-known fact that light for the mind, love for the heart and understanding for the intellect are the three conditions that must be satisfied in every man before he has real peace.

There is a pathway of wisdom and illumination for every human, which begins in any one of his incarnation on this earth and thereafter leads inward, for it is the pathway of consciousness and spiritual realisation leading ever inward, more inward toward the mystic East, which is the heart of the universe and the core, the rising sun of spiritually divine consciousness. This path to the heart of the universe is one and yet different for every human being. Every human being himself is journeying on that pathway based on his own mental process and the strength of belief and intensity of his yearning. It is built of the stuff of nature's heart. It is the road on which the person has the nature's streaming current of energy within him, and following this road he reaches perfection in due time; but this is the road of long-enduring slow evolution, moving ahead little by little in each life, through the incalculable ages. But once the soul finds its track, it is easy to walk forward birth by birth.

Another method of attaining truth and enlightenment is the one that the Great Ones of human race have followed. It is the quick road, but a steep one. It is the road of self-conquest, the road of giving up of self for All, the road by which a personal man becomes the impersonal Buddha, the impersonal Christ; the road by which love for self is abandoned, and the whole being is filled with love for all things both large and small. It is the road of initiation, steep and thorny pathway to the gods.

In the Orient there have been four different paths of self-realisation that the four classes of the society had been following. These four pathways correspond very accurately with the four grades, social and political, of the early civilizations of India since the Vedic period: the Shudra, the agriculturist; the Vaishya, the commercial man; the Kshatriya, the administrator, the warrior, the king, the prince and fourth, the Brahmana, the philosopher, the sage.

Among these four pathways, the first is Karma Marga, the 'path of action' that stresses on the salvation by works. The second is Bhakti Marga, the 'path of devotion' that believes in salvation by faith. These two paths or these two systems are known for improving the heart and mind of men and have been respectively called salvation by works, and salvation by faith. But these two paths are not the highest. The third path is Raja-yoga marga, the 'path of raja-yoga': the path which the striving entity follows in order to attain freedom and light ultimately gaining the union with the self within by means of self-devised efforts. And the fourth path, considered to be for the choicest of men, is called Jnana Marga, the 'wisdom path': the path of the great seers and sages, which is the noblest portion of mankind.

The Karma path is actually a style of leading life in accordance with the principles of the Holy Scriptures following the exact methods that are designated for each class of the society. The Bhakti path is the path of true worship of the Supreme, to such a limit that the ecstasy of the human soul is attained.

The Raja yoga path is quite a difficult one because it is followed by a series of practises to tame the human heart, mind and body to walk uninterruptedly on the pathway to enlightenment. This includes several daily practises:

1. Asana

A man wishes to control his mind, to be able to think one chosen thought for as long as he wishes without interruption. For this the first difficulty arises from the body, which keeps on asserting its presence. He person therefore wants to stretch, scratch or sneeze. This nuisance is so persistent that the Hindus have devised a special practice for quieting it. The word Asana literally means "posture." One of the highest authorities of spiritual practises is the ancient sage Patanjali. He says, 'Asana is that which is firm and pleasant.' In a sense this is true, because any posture becomes uncomfortable sooner or later. The steadiness and easiness mark a definite attainment.

2. Pranayama and Mantrayoga

For the ultimate goal of meditation being to still the mind, it may be considered a useful preliminary to still consciousness of all the functions of the body. Some meditators carry it to the point of trying to stop the beating of the heart. Pranayama deals with the timing of breathing according to one's own will. The best way for doing it is by the using a mantra. The mantra is a sequence of spiritual words for continuous chanting. The thought is bound down to a recurring cycle of reciting and any intruding thoughts are thrown off by the mantra, just as pieces of putty would be from a fly-wheel; and the swifter the chanting is done, the more difficult it is for any thought to stick to the mind.

Pranayama is very useful in quieting the emotions, thoughts and appetites of human mind and body. Whether it is by reason of the mechanical pressure that it asserts, or by the thorough combustion that it assures in the lungs but it is admirable from the standpoint of health. Digestive troubles in particular are very easy to remove in this way. It purifies both the body and the lower functions of the mind.

3. Yama and Niyama

The Hindu philosophy has placed these two attainments in the forefront of their programme. They are the 'moral qualities' and the 'good works' that are supposed to induce mental tranquillity. "Yama" consists of non-killing, truthfulness, non-stealing and non-receiving of any gift. The commandments of Moses are also the same and so are the one given by Christ. The 'non-receiving of gifts,' for instance, is quite important for a Hindu, who would be thoroughly upset for weeks if any one gave him something. But an average European takes things as they come by the time.

4. Pratyahara

This is the first process in the mental part. The previous practices of Asana, Pranayama, Yama, and Niyama, have been the acts of the body, while Pratyahara is purely mental. Pratyahara is introspection, a sort of general examination of the contents of the mind that we wish to control. After Asana had been mastered, all immediate exciting causes get removed, and then the person feels free to think of what he thinks.

5. Dharana

This practise deals with the gathering together of all the powers of the mind, in order to be able to focus them on one single point. According to Patanjali, 'Dhrana is holding the mind on to some particular object.'

6. Dhyana

The Hindus speak of Dhyana as a lesser form of Samadhi. Patanjali says that while Dhrana is holding the mind on to some particular object, Dhyana is an unbroken flow of knowledge in that subject. So Dhyana may be considered as a result rather than as a method. The most important factor in Dhyana is the dissolving of one's Ego.

7. Samadhi

The ancient scriptures say, 'By Pranayama impurities of the body are thrown out; by Dharana the impurities of the mind; by Pratyahara the impurities of attachment; and by Samadhi is taken off everything that hides the lordship of the soul.' Literally, 'Sam' in Greek means 'together with,' while 'Adhi' means 'Lord,' and so a reasonable translation of the whole word would be 'Union with the God,' which is also the exact term used by Christian mystics to describe their attainment. Dhyana resembles Samadhi in many respects. But in Samadhi, there is a union of the ego and the non-ego, and a loss of the senses of time and space and causality.

Ancient Greeks followed a different system of teaching. There were three states that a person in his quest for mysticism was supposed to pass successfully. First came the 'theophanic' mystery, which was the appearance at the solemn moment of initiation of man's own inner god to himself. The second was called '*theopneusty*', which is a Greek compound word meaning 'the inbreathing of a god.' In it man remained conscious of his inner divinity by inner as well as outer senses. As such he felt the inspiration flowing through his intellectual and spiritual veins that became permanent with the passing of time. Finally, there came the most sublime mystery of all, called '*theopathy' which literally means* 'the suffering a god.' This was actually symbolic to a state in which the person suffered himself to become a truly selfless channel of communication of his own inner god, his own higher self. This practise is even today common among the Sufis and other mystic schools of India.

Related branches

With the passing of time, many enlightened saints added to the knowledge of Esotericism all over the world. This led to the development of certain occult sciences that indeed had their roots in the principles of Esotericism. One of such sciences is Astrology. This science had been totally based on intuition that in turns forms the basis of the esoteric philosophy.

Great sages of ancient times laid down certain principles of thought and of study that represent fundamental operations and characteristic natures of the universe and the forces of nature. And no one of them ever attempted to teach of these operations and natures as one would teach a language or a mere physical science. Rather they hinted people by an appeal to intuition and innate knowledge. They led people step by step until finally they saw the hidden meaning that was conveyed as a key. They finally taught how to grasp and apply that key depending on their pupil's own spiritual insight.

The present day's so called astrological teachers have materialised this science. Now- a-days they print pamphlets and books, and cast and read the horoscope. Occasionally, by a lucky hit or a happy guess which is of course guided more or less by the fragments of ancient knowledge that have come down to us through the ancient scriptures, some points may get correct. Astrology of the ancients was indeed a great and noble science. Modern astrology is but the tattered and rejected outer coating of real ancient astrology. Astrology was the doctrine of origin, of nature, of destiny, of solar bodies, of planetary bodies, and of the beings that dwell on them. This wonderful science was founded on two doctrines mainly: the doctrine of the spheres, and the doctrine of the circulations of the cosmos. And the so-called astrology that has come down to us and is with us today is a series of incomplete and mutilated fragments of teachings misunderstood by the later Greeks and Romans themselves. The term astrology means the 'science of the celestial bodies.' So great and so noble was it that it was held strictly as a Mystery-teaching.

Ancient nations themselves forbade the public practice and teaching of astrology, because they knew that it could not be taught or practiced honestly in public as a means of private gain. They even went so far in the Roman Empire as to forbid its practice under penalty of banishment or death. The Mediterranean nations also issued strict laws against the 'Chaldaeans' or 'astrologers.'

The Old Testament is also full of allusions to the twelve zodiacal signs, and the whole scheme is built upon it such as heroes, personages, and events. Thus in the dream of Joseph, who saw eleven 'stars' bowing to the *twelfth*, which was *his* 'star,' symbolises the zodiac itself. The Roman Catholics later discovered in it a prophecy of Christ, who is that twelfth star along with the eleven apostles; the absence of the twelfth was also regarded as a prophetic allusion to the treachery of Judas. The twelve sons of Jacob are again a reference to the same

Real astrology is a very profound truth, for there actually is a bond of closest union, a strict and perfect correspondence among all the parts of being forming one vast organism through which circulates and flows one universal life throughout the cosmic. This life follows certain channels, and collects in certain centres, and these channels and centres are filled with spiritual and intellectual energies. These forces function in the centers, certain solar systemic abodes called the planets, and here lies the secret of the circulations, the secret of the gravitational pull which draws the life-atoms of the cosmos here and not there, or vice versa.

The Power within Human Body

Man is considered to be a focus of creative powers since ancient times. He is said to be a generating point of energies that are constantly being thrown forth from him in the form of innumerable streams and rivers, of little lives. It is only through his physical emanations that these atomic lives, these life-atoms, flow from the body. Similarly they leave the mind too. In mind these are in the form of thoughts, which are thus cast into the thought-atmosphere of cosmic. Each thought is an entity, because it could not have existed even for a fraction of a second if it did not have an individuality of some kind inhering in it and composing its essence.

These streams of emanations pass into invisible realms as thoughts; and into the physical, visible realms as physical emanations. But all the invisible ones, the thoughts good, bad, indifferent, highly colored, almost colourless, highly emotional, cold, hot, clean, sweet, infamous, all kinds of energies leave man's mind and it is these life-atoms, which begin to evolve on their own account, and in time become the intermediate nature of animals as they so evolve in their future births.

Man's such emanations already build up the animal world; the animals feed on these life-atoms. Similarly the sun also pours forth its vital essence in space, giving life and energy and ethereal substance to all that its lively rays touch, as well as its own atoms, its electrons belonging to the physical sphere. That might be the reason of the ancient Hindu tradition of pouring water towards the sun every morning. Sending thought atoms for producing a soothing effect.

As man continuously pours forth his vitality. These life-streams oozing out of him give life and evolutionary impulse and characteristics to the entities of the kingdoms below humans, because these subhuman kingdoms are actually the evolved derivatives of the thoughts and vital emanations of human race. Man's thoughts of hate and antagonism, his beastly passions, and various negative energies which flow forth from him, are the roots of the things and entities in the subhuman kingdoms which man considers to be inimical and antagonistic to his own kingdom. So in reality these are the exact prototype of men's own hidden negativity and darker side. On the other hand, the harmonious, kindly, amiable, symmetrical, productive acts provide the psychical principles of the harmless, and shapely beasts, as well as the large range of medicinal plants, herbs and flowers of beauty and all the usefulness in the vegetable kingdom.

Our thoughts and desires, whether pure or impure, rule our lives and also our destinies. As we desire and we think, so we are and so we become. For thoughts and desires are things and they follow the law of nature. Our inmost thoughts and our heart's desires are our prayers whether good or evil and the law of karma sees to it that these prayers are granted.

As we know that nature is one vast organism therefore, everything in it is connected with everything else. No living being can breathe, no one can think, without setting in motion energies, forces, which ultimately reach to the utmost limits of our home universe, and pass beyond those limits to the frontiers of other universes. Therefore, even a thought about a star touches that star in due course of time, with infinitesimal effect. This is a truth that makes one reflect the emotions and feelings and mood.

The stars are perturbed even by our thoughts. Persons whose inner vision is more opened and who realize that the glorious luminaries scattered over the blue vault of night are physical garments of an inner and brilliant flame of consciousness, manifest as the splendour of these cosmic suns in quite a similar fashion as our consciousness manifests us as a human being. While those who have begun on the path to become a seer of the secrets of the cosmic, their thoughts reach the suns and the stars. Every one is a child of the sun therefore every atom of spiritual energy reaches its destination sooner or later.

Whatever bears the quality or character of any of the five evil passions – lust, anger, greed, vanity and attachment – or which in any manner hinders the soul in its progress towards spiritual freedom is wrong. So there is essentially a need to observe caution in the growth of wrong thoughts.

Death and Old age

According to esoteric philosophy, old age is a blessing, if the previous life has been lived morally. It brings an unattainable expansion of consciousness which youth knows nothing of. It brings with it increased intellectual power that the youth, the man of middle age, does not understand. The older man is nearer to the truth and sees more than does the still unseeing eye of the youth. A fine old age brings an expansion of soul, not only of the intellect but of the spiritual consciousness and also its vision. It is the time when all the bodily desires have been extinguished and it is the time when no passion kindles the heart. According to the esoteric philosophy, it is said that some time should be devoted to think beyond. Beyond this body, beyond this world searching for the true pathway to the true spiritual abode of eternal bliss.

But sometimes, when youthful life had been spent in satisfying physical desires; then even in age death is painful, because the natural withdrawal of soul from the body does not take place to such an extent as to calm down the pain, nor is the physical age attained so great before death finally comes. In actual, old age is nothing to fear. It is a blessing. It is the splendour of the life beyond, the higher life, the life in which higher incarnating ego thrives. Shadows of the coming events cast their shadows before. Similarly, the shadow of splendour after death is a fine old age.

Any human being can avoid a painful old age, or can surely reduce its pains. This can be attained by living humanly, by living in higher self, instead of idealising the wants and desires of the body. So when the old age approaches, it turns vibrant with the harmonies of another world, and beautiful with its visions of truth and glory. Death is an opener, the one giving vision; death is the greatest and loveliest change that the heart of nature has in store for us. Death to our old ones comes in peace and quiet, stealing like an angel of mercy into their being, releasing the bonds binding the soul to its vehicle of flesh; and the passage is as quiet and gentle as the coming of the twilight preceding night, and it is certainly a blessed sleep. Death is change, even as birth is through reincarnation, which is death to the soul, is change; there is no difference between death and life. The difference only lies in the change of another phase of life. Death is a phase of life even as life is a 'hase of death. It is the nature's rule that every physical body should sleep for a certain period in order to recuperate its forces, its powers; so must the psychical constitution of man have its rest time in God's land. Death is the portal through which the pilgrim enters a higher stage.

As we all sleep in bed for a night's rest and wake up fresh after regaining our strength. In exactly the similar fashion death also ensues the time when our physical bodies are laid down and finally dropped off into some mysterious wonderland to rise up again with a fresh energy to take up the tasks of our karmic life in a new human body.

Death is an absolute sleep, a perfect sleep; a perfect repose while sleep is an incomplete death, an imperfect death. We incarnate anew every time when we awake, whether from sleep or from death. It is said so because awaking means that the entity that temporarily has left the body during sleep, returns into that body, incarnates itself itself anew,Uthus the body awakens with the psychical fire again fills the blood, tissues and the nerves with energy. As also Maulana Rum said in all truth:

'Rise you, O soul, and come up before your death,
And behold your kingdom and your Eternal Home,
You are such that besides this body you have another body,
Do not therefore be afraid of getting out of the mortal frame.'

Concept of Heaven and Hell

There is no great religion of ancient times which does not teach the existence of certain forces of reward or of retribution, acting after man's death in appropriate spheres in which the so called soul of man meets with retribution, as some say, 'punishment' or 'reward' after physical death. Those spheres in which the soul receives purgative punishment are called hells in English tongue; and those in which the soul receives appropriate repose and reward are commonly called heavens. Jesus, in the Gospel 'according to John,' says the following, "In my Father's house are many mansions: if it were not so, I would have told you. I go there to prepare a place for you." He said this in the long final address that he gave to his disciples before his arrest and appearance before the authorities, according to the Christian legends.

According to esoteric philosophy, when a body breaks up at physical death the astral elements remain in the 'shadow-world' with the same conscious centre as in life. There the elements cling with the astral bodies and vitalise them as before. When the 'second death,' after that of the physical body, takes place the higher part of it withdraws into itself and takes the so-called human soul with it. The mind then becomes the spiritual monad of man. This human monad goes to the 'god-land' or 'god-country.' There are many degrees in 'god-lands': the highest, the intermediate, and the lowest.

The heavens constitute the highest parts of 'god-land' and the hells belong to the lowest parts of it. There is also a theory of Nirvana that is often discussed in Buddhist scriptures. This Nirvana is a very different thing from the heavens. Nirvana is a state of eternal bliss, a state of absorption in pure being, and is the destiny of those who have reached superhuman knowledge and purity and spiritual enlightenment.

The esoteric doctrine says that there is no such thing as punishment nor there is reward. It believes that after death each entity is drawn to the appropriate sphere to which the karmic destiny of the entity magnetically attracts it. Therefore as a man works, as a man sows, in his life, that and that only shall he reap in his life after death.

Rebirth

Rebirth is considered as an awakening from the rest between earth lives. It is the result of destiny, the destiny that has been formed in past lives. According to Esotericism, there are various causes of rebirth. First is men's quest for truth and eternal bliss. It is the never-ending curiosity of knowing the unknown. The instincts of men tell them the truth, but the common minds do not know to interpret them. Their minds, their intellects, are distorted through the teachings brought to them by those who have sought for light in the material world alone. And even if he is under the influence of materialism, he should keep his mind open to study the process of nature and cosmic. This may help him regain a higher sphere some day in future.

Man being an essential part of the universe must obey the cosmic law of re-embodiment: birth, then growth, then youth, then maturity, then expansion of faculty and power, then decay, then the coming of the great peace, the death sleep, rest; and then again the coming forth anew into existence. This is a universal truth and the universe, the galaxies, the planets and other celestial bodies are also bound by this rule of nature. Each one is a body; each one is an inseparable portion of the boundless universe, as all are. Each one springs forth from the womb of boundless space as its child and one universal cosmic law runs through all, so what happens to one, big or small, advanced or non-advanced, evolved or non-evolved, happens to everyone without exception.

Secondly, we carve our own destiny; making our self what we are. Our present state of existence is what in past lives we have made our self to be; and similarly the future will be what we are now making as we live our lives on earth and later in the invisible realms of the spaces of space.

The third cause resides in the bosom of each one of us. It is the thirst for material life, thirst for life on earth, hunger for the pastures and fields wherein once we had wandered and which are familiar to us. This unquenched thirst for pleasure and happiness brings us back to earth again and again. If one wishes to breakthrough this cycle, he has got to seek truth inside his own self.

The soul, after death and before returning to rebirth on earth, goes wherever its sum total of yearnings, emotions, aspirations, direct it to go. When a man casts this physical body off as a garment that has outworn its usefulness, he is attracted to those inner spheres and planes, which during the life on earth, last lived, had attracted him. The material yearnings, material hungers and thirsts, latent as seeds in character after death. These sweeter seeds of character, the fruitage, the consequence of our yearnings for beauty and for harmony and for peace, carry us into the realms where harmony and beauty and peace are found. These realms are spheres just as earth, but far more ethereal and far more beautiful. The eye of spirit sees more clearly. Death releases from one world, and passes through the portals of change into another world, precisely the same as the inverse takes place when the incarnating soul leaves the realms of finer ether to come down to our own grosser and material earth life into a heavy body of physical matter. Thus the eternal pilgrim passes through another stage on its everlasting journey towards perfection; and these changes take place one after another, before the next incarnation on the returning wheel of the cycle. With the pilgrim passing from one sphere to another through the revolving centuries, ever going higher, to superior realms, until the topmost point of the cycle of that particular pilgrim's journey is reached. As also Omar Khayyam's Rubaiyat says in all truth:

> 'It is but a Tent where takes his one day's rest
> A Sultan to the realm of Death addressed
> The Sultan rises, and the dark Farrash
> Strikes, and prepares it for another Guest.'

CONCLUSION

There are numerous examples before us that show that whatever era it has been, all the great spiritual teachers were not easily welcomed in the society. The great Socrates who, though not initiated conveyed parts of Mysteries to public ear, from his own intuitional insight and thus committed a serious crime. The legends concerning Jesus tell the same story. Every one of those great souls who have attempted to enlighten mankind throughout different ages was prosecuted and misunderstood, though every one of them was giving his lifework, his very soul, in order to help his fellows; every one of them was hated. But does that stop the Great souls to avoid taking birth in this world? No it never happened because the Higher being, the Supreme, the Eternal True always sends the positive vibrations in the form of Prophets to guide people on the pathway to their spiritual abode of eternal bliss.

Even if we search the literature of the Southern School of Buddhism, commonly called the Hinayana, or whether we turn to the more mystical elaboration of Lord Buddha's teaching as found in Central and Northern Asia, called the Mahayana, in both the cases we discover new visions of Reality with each new spiritual and intellectual effort of the mind. Buddhism in its northern school has as strong and vital an inner meaning of Esotericism, embodied in its various scriptural writings, as has any other of the great ancient world-religion.

In reference to the Esoteric Tradition that essentially forms the basis ofBuddhism and Hinduism, the fact remains unchallenged that in its higher strivings to attain Truth, the human mind is so intuitive and urgent, that it makes contact through the minds of those outstanding examples of human philosophical and religious genius. But it is to India, the so called 'Motherland of religions and philosophies,' that one should turn to find the best and most open examples of the systems of the Esoteric Tradition which during the last three or four millenniums has spread its influence not only throughout Asia of these eras, but it has been affecting more strongly with each passing century the great peoples of the West.

****

GLOSSARY

Aesma Daeva: The demon of lust and anger, wrath and revenge according to Zoroastrian mythology.

Agas: The demon of illness according to Zoroastrian mythology.

Ahura Mazda: The supreme creator god according to Zoroastrian mythology.

Ahurani: Female Yazads presiding over water in Zoroastrian mythology.

Airyaman: the god presiding over marriage according to Zoroastrian mythology.

Aka Manah: One of the Daevas and also the personification of sensual desire according to Zoroastrian mythology.

Akhshti: Yazad personifying peace in Zoroastrian mythology.

Allatum: The goddess of the underworld according to Zoroastrian mythology.

Ameretat: The feminine immortal of immortality according to Zoroastrian mythology.

Amesha Spentas: The highest spiritual beings created by Ahura Mazda according to

Zoroastrian mythology.

Anaghra Raocha: Yazad of the 'endless light' in Zoroastrian mythology.

Anahita: The goddess of water, fertility war and also a patroness of women according to Zoroastrian mythology.

Angra Mainyu: The god of darkness, the eternal destroyer of good, personification and creator of evil, bringer of death and disease according to Zoroastrian mythology.

Apam-natat: The god of water according to Zoroastrian mythology.

Apaosa: A demon that brings drought and aridity according to Zoroastrian mythology.

Apu Illapu: The Incan rain giver god.

Aredvi Sura Anahita: Female Yazad personifying water in Zoroastrian mythology

Armaiti: The feminine immortal of piety according to Zoroastrian mythology.

Arshtat: Female Yazad personifying rectitude or justice in Zoroastrian mythology.

Asana: A sitting posture helping in concentration.

Asha: The masculine immortal of the knowledge of the law of God according to Zoroastrian mythology.

Ashi Vanghuhi: Female Yazad presiding over blessings in Zoroastrian mythology.

Asman: Yazad presiding over the sky in Zoroastrian mythology.

Asto Vidatu: The demon of death according to Zoroastrian mythology.

Atar: The god of fire and purity, son of Ahura Mazda according to Zoroastrian mythology.

Atoseka: The male katcina in Hopi religion.

Baga: An epithet of the Supreme Being Ahura Mazda according to Zoroastrian mythology.

Bahram: The god of the planets and victory according to Zoroastrian mythology.

Balilokon: The great water snake in Hopi mythology.

Bhakti Marga: Sanskrit word denoting the 'path of devotion' that believes in salvation by faith.

Boi Machi: A ceremony associated with the worshipping of the fires, five times each day in Zoroastrianism.

Brahmana: The philosopher division of Vedic society.

Burijas: A war god according to Zoroastrian mythology.

Bushyasta: The yellow demon of lethargy and sloth according to Zoroastrian mythology.

Buyasta: The demon of laziness according to Zoroastrian mythology.

Canca: A maize pudding distributed during Inca sun festival

Centeotl: An Aztec male maize-spirit.

Chalchihuitlicue: The wife of Aztec god, Tlaloc.

Chasca: The Incan name of planet Venus.

Chicomecohuatl: The Aztec chief goddess of maize.

Chisti: Female Yazad personifying religious wisdom in Zoroastrian mythology.

Citlalpol or Tlauizcalpantecutli: The Aztec name of planet Venus.

Cotukinuniwa: A good and wise spirit in Hopi mythology.

Coya: The Incan queen.

Daena: Female Yazad presiding over the religion, Inner Self or Conscience in Zoroastrian mythology.

Daevas: The demons causing plagues and diseases and fighting against every form of religion according to Zoroastrian mythology.

Dahm: Yazad honoured on the fourth day after death in Zoroastrian mythology.

Dahma Afriti: The embodiment of power of benediction in Zoroastrian mythology.

Damoish Upamana: Yazad personifying anathema in Zoroastrian mythology.

Dena: A goddess, daughter of Ahura Mazda according to Zoroastrian mythology.

Dev: A demon of enormous power, a ruthless and immoral god of war according to Zoroastrian mythology.

Dhaka: The god of death and demon of deceit and mendacity according to Zoroastrian mythology.

Dharana: Sanskrit word denoting concentration on some subject.

Dhyana: Sanskrit word denoting an unbroken flow of knowledge from the higher realms.

Drug: A female demon, the representation of lying according to Zoroastrian mythology

Drvaspa: The goddess protecting cattle, children, and friendship according to Zoroastrian mythology.

Erethe: Female Yazad personifying truth in Zoroastrian mythology.

Esoteric: The secret doctrine.

Fravashis: The Guardian Angels in Zoroastrian mythology.

Gandarewa: A water-demon in Zoroastrian mythology.

Gaw: Yazad personifying cattle in Zoroastrian mythology.

Geush Urvan: The personification of all animal life in Zoroastrian mythology.

Geus-Tasan: The divine creator of cattle according to Zoroastrian mythology.

Haoma: The personification of the legendary Soma-plant according to Zoroastrian mythology.

Haptoiringa: A star Yazad, associated with Ursa Major in Zoroastrian mythology.

Haurvatat: The feminine immortal of wholeness or perfection according to Zoroastrian mythology.

Havani: Yazad presiding over the second watch of each day in Zoroastrian mythology.

Huitzilopochtli: The bloodthirsty Aztec god of war.

Huruing Wuhti: The Hopi goddess of creation.

Hvarekhshaeta: The many-horsed sun god according to Zoroastrian mythology.

Indar: The god of warfare, courage and bravery according to Zoroastrian mythology.

Indra: One of the seven Daevas and personification of apostasy according to Zoroastrian mythology.

Inti: The Incan sun god.

Ixtlilton: The Aztec god of medicine and healing.

Izha: The goddess of the sacrifice according to Zoroastrian mythology.

Jashan: The Thanksgiving and Memorial Ceremony of the Zoroastrian people.

Jnana Marga: Sanskrit word denoting the 'wisdom path.'

Juan de Onate: Governor and colonizer of New Mexico.

Kahope: An evil person opposite to Hopi.

Karma Marga: Sanskrit word denoting the 'path of action' that stresses on the salvation by works.

Kachina: Small wooden painted images used by Hopis in worship.

Khwarenah: Yazad presiding over Divine Grace or Fortune in Zoroastrian mythology.

Kshathra: The masculine immortal of loving service according to Zoroastrian mythology.

Kshatriya: The administrative division of Vedic society.

Kusti: The sacred string in Zoroastrianism.

Lpalnemohuani: The Aztec Sun god.

Macuilxochitl: The Aztec god of luck.

Mah: The god of the moon according to Zoroastrian mythology.

Mahat: Sanskrit word denoting Cosmic Ideation or Intelligence.

Mama-Kilya: the Incan Moon Mother and the wife of sun god.

Manthra Spenta: Yazad embodying the Holy Word in Zoroastrian mythology.

Mao: A moon god according to Zoroastrian mythology.

Maonghah: Yazad presiding over the Moon in Zoroastrian mythology.

Masau'u: The Hopi god of death.

Masi and Masyani: the first human couple according to Zoroastrian mythology.

Metztli or Yohualticitl: The Aztec goddess of the moon.

Mictlan or Mictlantecutli: The Aztec god of the dead.

Mithra: The god of light, contracts and friendship according to Zoroastrian mythology.

Mixcoatl: The Aztec god of chase.

Nairyosangha: The Messenger of the Supreme Ahura Mazda to mankind according to Zoroastrian mythology.

Nanahuatl: The Aztec god of skin diseases.

Nanghaithya: The personification of discontentment according to Zoroastrian mythology.

Navjote: The ceremony when the children are initiated into Zoroastrianism.

Neriosang: A Messenger-god according to Zoroastrian mythology.

Nirvana: Sanskrit word denoting a state of eternal bliss.

Niyama: Sanskrit word denoting good, pious deeds.

NoRoz (New Year): The highest festival of the year for Zoroastrians.

Omacatl: The Aztec god of festivity and joy.

Ometecutli and Omeciuatl: The Aztec father and mother of the whole human race.

Omow: The female katcina in Hopi religion.

Opochtli: The Aztec god sacred to the fishers and bird-catchers.

Paca-Mama: The Incan mother earth.

Paoiryaenis: Star Yazad associated with the Pleiades in Zoroastrian mythology.

Parbrahma: Sanskrit word denoting the 'Absolute.'

Parendi: Female Yazad of abundance in Zoroastrian mythology.

Paurwanya: Star Yazad associated with a constellation of uncertain identity in Zoroastrian mythology.

Peris: The Spirits of great beauty guiding mortals on their way to the Land of the Blessed, according to Zoroastrian mythology.

Pralaya: Sanskrit word denoting destruction of all life forms.

Pranayama: The timing of breath according to will.

Pratyahara: Sanskrit word denoting introspection of one's mind.

Quetzalcoatl: The Aztec god of heavens.

Quipu: Knotted threads used by the Incas to keep account of their dynasties.

Rahasya: Sanskrit word meaning esoteric doctrine or mystery.

Raja-yoga marga: Sanskrit word denoting the 'path of raja-yoga' that believes in union with the self within by means ot self-devised efforts.

Raman: Yazad presiding over Joy or Felicity in Zoroastrian mythology.

Rapithwin: The ancient god of midday according to Zoroastrian mythology.

Rapithwin: Yazad presiding over the period of the dayfrom noon to mid-afternoon in Zoroastrian mythology.

Rasanstat: Female Yazad personifying truth in Zoroastrian mythology.

Rashnu: The Zoroastrian divine angel of justice and last judgement and the personification of righteousness in Zoroastrian mythology.

Rata: Female Yazad personifying charity in Zoroastrian mythology.

Samadhi: Sanskrit word denoting union of mind with God.

Satavaesa: A star Yazad in Zoroastrian mythology.

Saurva: One of the seven main Daevas according to Zoroastrian mythology.

Shudra: The agriculturist division of Vedic society.

Soyal: The most sacred of all Hopi ceremonies.

Spider woman: The creator of evil people in Hopi mythology.

Sraosa: The personification of obedience and the messenger of the great god Ahura Mazda according to Zoroastrian mythology.

Sraosha: A spirit being who guards the soul for three days after death in Zoroastrian mythology.

Sudrah: The sacred shirt in Zoroastrianism.

Tenochtitlan: Ancient name of Mexico City.

Tepeyollotl or Tepeolotlec: The Aztec god of seismic disturbances and earthquakes.

Tezcatlipoca: The Aztec god with the burning and destroying power of the sun.

Thwasha: Personification of Infinite Space in Zoroastrian mythology.

Tishtrya: Yazad presiding over the star Sirius. Tishtrya also directs the rain in Zoroastrian mythology.

Tishtryaeinis: Star Yazad associated with Canis Minor in Zoroastrian mythology.

Tlaloc: The Aztec god of rain and moisture.

Tlalocan: The abode of Aztec god, Tlaloc.

Tlazolteotl: The Aztec goddess of desire and luxury.

Totec: The Aztec minor Sun god.

Upanishads: Ancient Sanskrit scriptures.

Ushah: Female Yazad of the dawn in Zoroastrian mythology.

Ushahin: Yazad presiding over the first watch of each day in Zoroastrian mythology.

Uzerin: Yazad presiding over the fourth watch of each day in Zoroastrian mythology.

Vaishya: The tradesman division of Vedic society.

Vanant: The guardian star of the west that conquers evil according to Zoroastrian mythology.

Vata: The god of the wind and one of the Yazatas in Zoroastrian mythology.

Vayu: The wind god according to Zoroastrian mythology.

Verethragna: The god of victory and the personification of aggressive triumph according to Zoroastrian mythology.

Villac Vmu: The Incan High-Priest.

Viracocha: the Incan supreme creator.

Visya: Yazad associated with the settlement in Zoroastrian mythology.

Vohu-Mana: The masculine immortal of love according to Zoroastrian mythology.

Vouruskasha: A heavenly lake that supplies water to the world according to Zoroastrian mythology.

Xipe: The Aztec god of fire, earth, and water.

Xiuhtecutli: The Aztec god of fire.

Xolotl: The Aztec god representing light flaming upward.

Yacatecutli: The Aztec god considered as the patron of travellers of the merchant class.

Yama: Sanskrit word denoting moral qualities.

Yazatas: The Angels, a created spiritual being, worthy of being honoured according to Zoroastrian mythology.

Yntip Raymi: The Incan festival of the Sun.

Zam: The deified earth according to Zoroastrian mythology.

Zam-Armatay: The goddess of earth according to Zoroastrian mythology.

Zantuma: Yazad presiding over the tribe in Zoroastrian mythology.

Zarich: A female member of the Daevas and the personification of ageing according to Zoroastrian mythology.

Zoroaster: The founder prophet of Zoroastrianism.

Zrvan Akarana: Personification of Boundless Time in Zoroastrian mythology.

****

BIBLIOGRAPHY

* Banerjee, G.N. Hellenism in Ancient India, Calcutta, 1920.
* Blavatsky, H.P. The Secret Doctrine, vol. 1 and vol. 2, Theosophical University Press.
* Brinton, D.G. The Sacred Songs of the Ancient Mexicans, 1890.
* Colton, H.S. Hopi Katchina Dolls, Albuquerque, 1949.
* Conze, E. Buddhism, its Essence and development, Oxford, 1953.
* Darmesteter, K. and Mills, L.H. The Zend Avesta, Oxford, 1880.
* Driver, Harold E. Indians of North America, University of Chicago Press, 1961.
* Encyclopaedia of Religion and Ethics, ed. J. Hastings, 13 vols., Edinburgh, 1908-26.
* Good News Bible, The Bible Society, 1994.
* Herodotus, The Histories, trans. A. de Selincourt, Harmondsworth, 1981.
* Joseph, Alice, Rosamond B. Spicer and Jane Chesky, The Desert People, University
* Keith, A.B. The Religion and Philosophy of the Vedas and Upanishads, Cambridge, 1925.
* Muller, F. M. The Upanishads, 2 vols. Oxford University Press, 1879-82.
* Muller, F. M. Vedic Hymns, 2 vols. Oxford, 1891-97.

* Oswalt, W.H. This Land was Theirs, John Wiley and sons, 1978.
* Pearce, Roy H. The Savages of America, Baltimore, 1965.
* Radhakrishnan, Sir S. Indian Philosophy, 2 vols. London, 1923-27.
* Rawlinson, H.G. Intercourse between India and the Western world, Cambridge, 1916.
* Stoherbatsky, T. Buddhist Logic, 2 vols. New York, 1962.
* The Bundahishn, Translated by E. W. West, Oxford University Press, 1897.
* The Rig Veda, Sanskriti Sansthan Press.
* Thompson, Laura and Alice Joseph, The Hopi Way, Chicago, 1944.
* Titiev, Mischa, The Hopi Indians of Old Oraibi, Ann Arbor, 1972.
* Tokarev, S. A History of Religion, Raduga Publications, 1989.
* Underhill, Ruth Murray. Red Man's America, University of Chicago Press, 1953.
* Vaillant, George. Aztecs of Mexico, Doran & Co. New York, 1941.
* Wissler, C. Indians of the United States, Natural History Library, 1966.
* Zarate, A. The Discovery and Conquest of Peru, Penguin Books.

****